The Reign of Andrew Jackson

Volume 20

By

Frederic Austin Ogg

Editor
Allen Johnson

Assistant Editors
Gerhard R. Lomer
Charles W. Jeffery's

Ross & Perry, Inc.
Washington, D.C.

Copyright 1919, Yale University Press
Reprinted by Ross & Perry, Inc. 2003
© Ross & Perry, Inc. 2003 on new material. All rights reserved.

Protected under the Berne Convention.

Printed in The United States of America

Ross & Perry, Inc. Publishers
216 G St., N.E.
Washington, D.C. 20002
Telephone (202) 675-8300
Facsimile (202) 675-8400
info@RossPerry.com

SAN 253-8555

Library of Congress Control Number: 2002109432
http://www.rossperry.com

ISBN 1-932109-02-1

Book Cover designed by Sapna. sapna@rossperry.com

☉ The paper used in this publication meets the requirements for permanence established by the American National Standard for Information Sciences "Permanence of Paper for Printed Library Materials" (ANSI Z39.48-1984).

All rights reserved. No copyrighted part of this publication may be reproduced, stored in a retrieval system, or transmitted, in any form or by any means, electronic, photocopying, recording, or otherwise, without the prior written permission of the publisher.

ANDREW JACKSON AS A FRONTIER LAWYER
From the painting by Stanley M. Arthurs

CONTENTS

I.	JACKSON THE FRONTIERSMAN	Page	1
II.	THE CREEK WAR AND THE VICTORY OF NEW ORLEANS	"	23
III.	THE "CONQUEST" OF FLORIDA	"	45
IV.	THE DEATH OF "KING CAUCUS"	"	68
V.	THE DEMOCRATIC TRIUMPH	"	95
VI.	THE "REIGN" BEGINS	"	113
VII.	THE WEBSTER-HAYNE DEBATE	"	137
VIII.	TARIFF AND NULLIFICATION	"	158
IX.	THE WAR ON THE UNITED STATES BANK	"	181
X.	THE REMOVAL OF THE SOUTHERN INDIANS	"	201
XI.	THE JACKSONIAN SUCCESSION	"	217
	BIBLIOGRAPHICAL NOTE	"	237
	INDEX	"	241

ILLUSTRATION

ANDREW JACKSON AS A FRONTIER LAWYER
  From the painting by Stanley M. Arthurs. *Frontispiece*

THE REIGN OF ANDREW JACKSON

CHAPTER I

JACKSON THE FRONTIERSMAN

AMONG the thousands of stout-hearted British subjects who decided to try their fortune in the Western World after the signing of the Peace of Paris in 1763 was one Andrew Jackson, a Scotch-Irish Presbyterian of the tenant class, sprung from a family long resident in or near the quaint town of Carrickfergus, on the northern coast of Ireland, close by the newer and more progressive city of Belfast.

With Jackson went his wife and two infant sons, a brother-in-law, and two neighbors with their families, who thus made up a typical eighteenth-century emigrant group. Arrived at Charleston, the travelers fitted themselves out for an overland journey, awaited a stretch of favorable weather.

2   THE REIGN OF ANDREW JACKSON

and set off for the Waxhaw settlement, one hundred and eighty miles to the northwest, where numbers of their kinsmen and countrymen were already established. There the Jacksons were received with open arms by the family of a second brother-in-law, who had migrated a few years earlier and who now had a comfortable log house and a good-sized clearing.

The settlement lay on the banks of the upper Catawba, near the junction of that stream with Waxhaw Creek; and as it occupied a fertile oasis in a vast waste of pine woods, it was for decades largely cut off from touch with the outside world. The settlement was situated, too, partly in North Carolina and partly in South Carolina, so that in the pre-Revolutionary days many of the inhabitants hardly knew, or cared to know, in which of the two provinces they dwelt.

Upon their arrival Jackson's friends bought land on the creek and within the bounds of the settlement. Jackson himself was too poor, however, to do this, and accordingly took up a claim six miles distant on another little stream known as Twelve-mile Creek. Here, in the fall of 1765, he built a small cabin, and during the winter he cleared five or six acres of ground. The next year he was able

JACKSON THE FRONTIERSMAN 3

to raise enough corn, vegetables, and pork to keep his little household from want. The tract thus occupied cannot be positively identified, but it lay in what is now Union County, North Carolina, a few miles from Monroe, the county seat.

Then came tragedy of a sort in which frontier history abounds. In the midst of his efforts to hew out a home and a future for those who were dear to him the father sickened and died, in March, 1767, at the early age of twenty-nine, less than two years after his arrival at the settlement. Tradition says that his death was the result of a rupture suffered in attempting to move a heavy log, and that it was so sudden that the distracted wife had no opportunity to seek aid from the distant neighbors. When at last the news got abroad, sympathy and assistance were lavished in true frontier fashion. Borne in a rude farm wagon, the remains were taken to the Waxhaw burying ground and were interred in a spot which tradition, but tradition only, is able today to point out.

The widow never returned to the desolated homestead. She and her little ones were taken into the family of one of her married sisters, where she spent her few remaining years. On the 15th of March, less than two weeks after her husband's

4   THE REIGN OF ANDREW JACKSON

death, she gave birth to a third son; and the child was promptly christened Andrew, in memory of the parent he would never know.

Curiously, the seventh President's birthplace has been a matter of sharp controversy. There is a tradition that the birth occurred while the mother was visiting a neighboring family by the name of McKemy; and Parton, one of Jackson's principal biographers, adduces a good deal of evidence in support of the story. On the other hand, Jackson always believed that he was born in the home of the aunt with whom his bereaved mother took up her residence; and several biographers, including Bassett, the most recent and the best, accept this contention. It really matters not at all, save for the circumstance that if the one view is correct Jackson was born in North Carolina, while if the other is correct he was born in South Carolina. Both States have persistently claimed the honor. In the famous proclamation which he addressed to the South Carolina nullifiers in 1832 Jackson referred to them as "fellow-citizens of my native state"; in his will he spoke of himself as a South Carolinian; and in correspondence and conversation he repeatedly declared that he was born on South Carolina soil. Jackson was far from infallible, even

JACKSON THE FRONTIERSMAN 5

in matters closely touching his own career. But the preponderance of evidence on the point lies decidedly with South Carolina.

No one, at all events, can deny to the Waxhaw settlement an honored place in American history. There the father of John C. Calhoun first made his home. There the Revolutionary general, Andrew Pickens, met and married Rebecca Calhoun. There grew up the eminent North Carolinian Governor and diplomat, William R. Davie. There William H. Crawford lived as a boy. And there Jackson dwelt until early manhood.

For the times, young Andrew was well brought up. His mother was a woman of strong character, who cherished for her last-born the desire that he should become a Presbyterian clergyman. The uncle with whom he lived was a serious-minded man who by his industry had won means ample for the comfortable subsistence of his enlarged household. When he was old enough, the boy worked for his living, but no harder than the frontier boys of that day usually worked; and while his advantages were only such as a backwoods community afforded, they were at least as great as those of most boys similarly situated, and they were far superior to those of the youthful Lincoln.

Jackson's earlier years, nevertheless, contained little promise of his future distinction. He grew up amidst a rough people whose tastes ran strongly to horse-racing, cockfighting, and heavy drinking, and whose ideal of excellence found expression in a readiness to fight upon any and all occasions in defense of what they considered to be their personal honor. In young Andrew Jackson these characteristics appeared in a superlative degree. He was mischievous, willful, daring, reckless. Hardly an escapade took place in the community in which he did not share; and his sensitiveness and quick temper led him continually into trouble. In his early teens he swore like a trooper, chewed tobacco incessantly, acquired a taste for strong drink, and set a pace for wildness which few of his associates could keep up. He was passionately fond of running foot races, leaping the bar, jumping, wrestling, and every sort of sport that partook of the character of mimic battle — and he never acknowledged defeat. "I could throw him three times out of four," testifies an old schoolmate, "but he would never *stay throwed*. He was dead game even then, and never *would* give up." Another early companion says that of all the boys he had known Jackson was the only bully who was not also a coward.

JACKSON THE FRONTIERSMAN 7

Of education the boy received only such as was put unavoidably in his way. It is said that his mother taught him to read before he was five years old; and he attended several terms in the little low-roofed log schoolhouse in the Waxhaw settlement. But his formal instruction never took him beyond the fundamentals of reading, writing, geography, grammar, and "casting accounts." He was neither studious nor teachable. As a boy he preferred sport to study, and as a man he chose to rely on his own fertile ideas rather than to accept guidance from others. He never learned to write the English language correctly, although he often wrote it eloquently and convincingly. In an age of bad spellers he achieved distinction from the number of ways in which he could spell a word within the space of a single page. He could use no foreign languages; and of the great body of science, literature, history, and the arts he knew next to nothing. He never acquired a taste for books, although vanity prompted him to treasure throughout his public career all correspondence and other documentary materials that might be of use to future biographers. Indeed, he picked as a biographer first his military aide, John Reid, and later his close friend, John H. Eaton, whom

8 THE REIGN OF ANDREW JACKSON

he had the satisfaction in 1829 of appointing Secretary of War.

When the Revolution came, young Andrew was a boy of ten. For a time the Carolina backwoods did not greatly feel the effect of the change. But in the spring of 1780 all of the revolutionary troops in South Carolina were captured at Charleston, and the lands from the sea to the mountains were left at the mercy of Tarleton's and Rawdon's bands of redcoats and their Tory supporters. Twice the Waxhaw settlement was ravaged before the patriots could make a stand. Young Jackson witnessed two battles in 1780, without taking part in them, and in the following year he, a brother, and a cousin were taken prisoners in a skirmish. To the day of his death Jackson bore on his head and hand the marks of a saber blow administered by a British lieutenant whose jack boots he refused to polish. When an exchange of prisoners was made, Mrs. Jackson secured the release of her two boys, but not until after they had contracted smallpox in Camden jail. The older one died, but the younger, though reduced to a skeleton, survived. Already the third brother had given up his life in battle; and the crowning disaster came when the mother, going as a volunteer to nurse the wounded

JACKSON THE FRONTIERSMAN 9

Waxhaw prisoners on the British vessels in Charleston harbor, fell ill of yellow fever and perished. Small wonder that Andrew Jackson always hated the British uniform, or that when he sat in the executive chair an anti-British feeling colored all of his dealings with foreign nations!

At the age of fourteen, the sandy-haired, pockmarked lad of the Waxhaws found himself alone in the world. The death of his relatives had made him heir to a portion of his grandfather's estate in Carrickfergus; but the property was tied up in the hands of an administrator, and the boy was in effect both penniless and homeless. The memory of his mother and her teachings was, as he was subsequently accustomed to say, the only capital with which he started life. To a natural waywardness and quarrelsomeness had been added a heritage of bitter memories, and the outlook was not bright.

Upon one thing the youth was determined: he would no longer be a charge upon his uncle or upon any one else. What to turn to, however, was not so easy to decide. First he tried the saddler's trade, but that was too monotonous. Then he undertook school-teaching; that proved little better. Desirous of a glimpse of the world, he went to Charleston in the autumn of 1782. There he made the

10 THE REIGN OF ANDREW JACKSON

acquaintance of some people of wealth and fell into habits of life which were beyond his means. At the race track he bet and swaggered himself into notice; and when he ran into debt he was lucky enough to free himself by winning a large wager. But the proceeds of his little inheritance, which had in the meantime become available, were now entirely used up; and when in the spring the young spendthrift went back to the Waxhaws, he had only a fine horse with elegant equipment, a costly pair of pistols, a gold watch, and a fair wardrobe — in addition to some familiarity with the usages of fashion — to show for his spent "fortune."

One other thing which Jackson may have carried back with him from Charleston was an ambition to become a lawyer. At all events, in the fall of 1784 he entered the law office of a certain Spruce Macay in the town of Salisbury, North Carolina; and, after three years of intermittent study, he was admitted to practice in the courts of the State. The instruction which he had received was not of a high order, and all accounts agree that the young man took his tasks lightly and that he learned but little law. That he fully sustained the reputation which he had gained in the Waxhaws is indicated by testimony of one of Macay's fellow townsmen,

JACKSON THE FRONTIERSMAN 11

after Jackson had become famous, to the effect that the former student had been "the most roaring, rollicking, game-cocking, card-playing, mischievous fellow that ever lived in Salisbury."

Upon his admission to the bar the irresponsible young blade hung out his shingle in Martinsville, Guilford County, North Carolina, and sat down to wait for clients. He was still less than twenty years old, without influence, and with only such friends as his irascible disposition permitted him to make and hold. Naturally business came slowly, and it became necessary to eke out a living by serving as a local constable and also by assisting in a mercantile enterprise carried on by two acquaintances in the town. After a year this hand-to-mouth existence began to pall. Neither then nor in later life did Jackson have any real taste or aptitude for law. He was not of a legal turn of mind, and he was wholly unprepared to suffer the sacrifices and disappointments which a man of different disposition would have been willing to undergo in order to win for himself an established position in his profession. Chagrin in this restless young man was fast yielding to despair when an alluring field of action opened for him in the fast-developing country beyond the mountains.

The settlement of white men in that part of North Carolina which lay west of the Alleghanies had begun a year or two after Jackson's birth. At first the hardy pioneers found lodgment on the Watauga, Holston, Nolichucky, and other streams to the east of modern Knoxville. But in 1779 a colony was planted by James Robertson and John Donelson on the banks of the Cumberland, two hundred miles farther west, and in a brief time the remoter settlement, known as Nashville, became a Mecca for homeseeking Carolinians and Virginians. The intervening hill and forest country abounded in hostile Indians. The settler or trader who undertook to traverse this region took his life in his hands, and the settlements themselves were subject to perennial attack.

In 1788, after the collapse of an attempt of the people of the "Western District" to set up an independent State by the name of Franklin, the North Carolina Assembly erected the three counties included in the Cumberland settlement into a superior court district; and the person selected for judge was a close friend of Jackson, John McNairy, who also had been a law pupil of Spruce Macay in Salisbury. McNairy had been in the Tennessee region two years, but at the time of receiving his

JACKSON THE FRONTIERSMAN 13

judicial appointment he was visiting friends in the Carolinas. His description of the opportunities awaiting ambitious young men in the back country influenced a half-dozen acquaintances, lawyers and others, to make the return trip with him; and among the number was Jackson. Some went to assume posts which were at McNairy's disposal, but Jackson went only to see the country.

Assembling at Morganton, on the east side of the mountains, in the fall of 1788, the party proceeded leisurely to Jonesboro, which, although as yet only a village of fifty or sixty log houses, was the metropolis of the eastern Tennessee settlements. There the party was obliged to wait for a sufficient band of immigrants to assemble before they could be led by an armed guard with some degree of safety through the dangerous middle country. As a highway had just been opened between Jonesboro and Nashville, the travelers were able to cover the distance in fifteen days. Jackson rode a fine stallion, while a pack mare carried his worldly effects, consisting of spare clothes, blankets, half a dozen law books, and small quantities of ammunition, tea, tobacco, liquor, and salt. For defense he bore a rifle and three pistols; and in his pocket he carried one

14 THE REIGN OF ANDREW JACKSON

hundred and eighty dollars of the much valued hard money. On the second day of November the emigrant train made its appearance in Nashville bringing news of much interest — in particular, that the Federal Constitution had been ratified by the ninth State, and that the various legislatures were preparing to choose electors, who would undoubtedly make George Washington the first President of the Republic.

Less than ten years old, Nashville had now a population of not over two hundred. But it was the center of a somewhat settled district extending up and down the Cumberland for a distance of eighty or ninety miles, and the young visitor from the Waxhaws quickly found it a promising field for his talents. There was only one lawyer in the place, and creditors who had been outbid for his services by their debtors were glad to put their cases in the hands of the newcomer. It is said that before Jackson had been in the settlement a month he had issued more than seventy writs to delinquent debtors. When, in 1789, he was appointed "solicitor," or prosecutor, in Judge McNairy's jurisdiction with a salary of forty pounds for each court he attended, his fortune seemed made and he forthwith gave up all thought of returning to his

JACKSON THE FRONTIERSMAN 15

Carolina home. Instead he took lodgings under the roof of the widow of John Donelson, and in 1791 he married a daughter of that doughty frontiersman. Land was still cheap, and with the proceeds of his fees and salary he purchased a large plantation called Hunter's Hill, thirteen miles from Nashville, and there he planned to establish a home which would take rank as one of the finest in the western country.

The work of a frontier solicitor was diverse and arduous. A turbulent society needed to be kept in order and the business obligations of a shifty and quarrelsome people to be enforced. No great knowledge of law was required, but personal fearlessness, vigor, and incorruptibility were indispensable. Jackson was just the man for the business. His physical courage was equaled by his moral strength; he was passionately devoted to justice; he was diligent and conscientious; and, as one writer has remarked, bad grammar, incorrect pronunciation, and violent denunciation did not shock the judges of that day or divert the mind of juries from the truth. Traveling almost constantly over the wretched roads and through the dark forests, dodging Indians, swimming his horse across torrential streams, sleeping alone in the woods with hand on rifle, threatened by desperate wrongdoers, Andrew Jackson became the best-known figure in all western Tennessee and won at this time a great measure of that public confidence which later became his chief political asset.

Meanwhile the rapid growth of population south of the Ohio River made necessary new arrangements for purposes of government. In 1790 the region between the Ohio and the present States of Alabama and Mississippi, having been turned over to the Nation by its earlier possessors, was erected into the "Southwest Territory," and in 1791 the northern half became the State of Kentucky. In 1793 the remainder of the Territory set up a Legislature, and three years later delegates from the eleven counties met at Knoxville to draw up a new frame of government with a view to admission to statehood. Jackson was a member of this convention, and tradition has it that it was he who brought about the selection of the name Tennessee, an Indian term meaning "The Great Crooked River," as against Franklin, Washington, and other proposed designations for the new State. At all events, upon the admission of the State in 1796, he was chosen as its sole representative in the lower branch of Congress.

In the late autumn of that year the young lawmaker set out for the national capital at Philadelphia, and there he arrived, after a journey of almost eight hundred miles on horseback, just as the triumphs of the Democrats in the recent presidential election were being duly celebrated. He had not been chosen as a party man, but it is altogether probable that his own sympathies and those of most of his constituents lay with the Jeffersonians; and his appearance on the floor of Congress was an omen of the fast-rising tide of western democracy which should never find its ultimate goal until this rough but honest Tennesseean should himself be borne into the presidential chair.

Jackson's career in Congress was brief and uneventful. After a year of service in the House of Representatives he was appointed to fill the unexpired term of William Blount in the Senate. But this post he resigned in 1798 in order to devote his energies to his private affairs. While at Philadelphia he made the acquaintance not only of John Adams, Jefferson, Randolph, Gallatin, and Burr, but of his future Secretary of State, Edward Livingston, and of some other persons who were destined to be closely connected with his later career. But Jackson was not fitted for a legislative

18 THE REIGN OF ANDREW JACKSON

body either by training or by temperament. He is recorded as speaking in the House only twice and in the Senate not at all, and he seems to have made no considerable impression upon his colleagues. Gallatin later described him as "a tall, lank, uncouth-looking personage, with long locks of hair hanging over his face, and a queue down his back tied in an eel-skin; his dress singular, his manners and deportment those of a rough backwoodsman." And Jefferson is represented as saying of Jackson to Webster at Monticello in 1824: "His passions are terrible. When I was president of the Senate he was Senator, and he could never speak on account of the rashness of his feelings. I have seen him attempt it repeatedly, and as often choke with rage."

Return to Tennessee meant, however, only a transfer from one branch of the public service to another, for the ex-Senator was promptly appointed to a judgeship of the state supreme court at a salary of six hundred dollars a year. The position he found not uncongenial and he retained it for six years. Now, as earlier, Jackson's ignorance of law was somewhat compensated by his common sense, courage, and impartiality; and while only one of his decisions of this period is extant, Parton

JACKSON THE FRONTIERSMAN 19

reports that the tradition of fifty years ago represented them as short, untechnical, unlearned, sometimes ungrammatical, but generally right. The daily life of Jackson as a frontier judge was hardly less active and exciting than it had been when he was a prosecuting attorney. There were long and arduous horseback journeys "on circuit"; illtempered persons often threatened, and sometimes attempted, to deal roughly with the author of an unfavorable decision; occasionally it was necessary to lay aside his dignity long enough to lend a hand in capturing or controlling a desperate character. For example, on arriving once in a settlement Jackson found that a powerful blacksmith had committed a crime and that the sheriff dared not arrest him. "Summon me," said the judge; whereupon he walked down from the bench, found the culprit, led him into court, and sentenced him.

In 1804 Jackson resigned his judgeship in order to give exclusive attention again to his private affairs. He had fallen badly into debt, and his creditors were pressing him hard. One expedient after another failed, and finally Hunter's Hill had to be given up. He saved enough from the wreck, however, to purchase a small plantation eight miles from Nashville; and there, after several years of

20 THE REIGN OF ANDREW JACKSON

financial rehabilitation, he erected the handsome brick house which the country came subsequently to know as "The Hermitage." In partnership with two of his wife's relatives, Jackson had opened a store in which, even while still a member of the highest tribunal of the State, he not infrequently passed tea and salt and calico over the counter to his neighbors. In small trading, however, he was not adept, and the store failed. Nevertheless, from 1804 until 1813 he successfully combined with planting and the stock-raising business enterprises of a larger sort, especially slave and horse dealing. His debts paid off, he now became one of the most prosperous, as he already was one of the most influential, men of the Cumberland country.

But it was not given to Andrew Jackson to be a mere money-maker or to dwell in quietness. In 1804 he was denied the governorship of the New Orleans Territory because he was described to Jefferson as "a man of violent passions, arbitrary in his disposition, and frequently engaged in broils and disputes." During the next decade he fully lived up to this description. He quarreled with Governor John Sevier, and only the intervention of friends prevented the two from doing each other violence. He broke off friendly relations with his old patron, Judge McNairy. In a duel he killed Charles Dickinson, who had spoken disparagingly of Mrs. Jackson, and he himself suffered a wound which weakened him for life. He publicly caned one Thomas Swann. In a rough-and-tumble encounter with Thomas Hart Benton and the latter's brother Jesse he was shot in the shoulder and one of his antagonists was stabbed. This list of quarrels, threats, fights, and other violent outbursts could be extended to an amazing length. "Yes, I had a fight with Jackson," Senator Benton admitted late in life; "a fellow was hardly in the fashion then who hadn't."

At the age of forty-five Jackson had not yet found himself. He was known in his own State as "a successful planter, a breeder and racer of horses, a swearer of mighty oaths, a faithful and generous man to his friends, a chivalrous man to women, a hospitable man at his home, a desperate and relentless man in personal conflicts, a man who always did the things he set himself to do." But he had achieved no nation-wide distinction; he had not wrought out a career; he had made almost as many enemies as friends; he had cut himself off from official connections; he had no desire to return to the legal profession; and he was so dissatisfied with his lot and outlook that he seriously considered moving to Mississippi in order to make a fresh start.

One thread, however, still bound him to the public service. From 1802 he had been major general of militia in the eleven counties of western Tennessee; and notwithstanding the fact that three calls from the Government during a decade had yielded no real opportunity for action, he clung both to the office and to the hope for a chance to lead his "hardy sons of the West" against a foe worthy of their efforts. This chance came sooner than people expected, and it led in precisely the direction that Jackson would have chosen — toward the turbulent, misgoverned Spanish dependency of Florida.

CHAPTER II

THE CREEK WAR AND THE VICTORY OF NEW ORLEANS

EVERY schoolboy knows and loves the story of the midnight ride of Paul Revere. But hardly anybody has heard of the twenty-day, fifteen-hundred-mile ride of "Billy" Phillips, the President's express courier, who in 1812 carried to the Southwest the news that the people of the United States had entered upon a second war with their British kinsmen. William Phillips was a young, lithe Tennesseean whom Senator Campbell took to Washington in 1811 as secretary. When not more than sixteen years old he had enjoyed the honor of riding Andrew Jackson's famous steed, Truxton, in a heat race, for the largest purse ever heard of west of the mountains, with the proud owner on one side of the stakes. In Washington he occasionally turned an honest penny by jockey-riding in the races on the old track of Bladensburg, and eventually he became one of a squad of ten or twelve expert

24 THE REIGN OF ANDREW JACKSON

horsemen employed by the Government in carrying urgent long-distance messages.

After much hesitation, Congress passed a joint resolution at about five o'clock on Friday, June 18, 1812, declaring war against Great Britain. Before sundown the express couriers were dashing swiftly on their several courses, some toward reluctant New England, some toward Pennsylvania and New York, some southward, some westward. To Phillips it fell to carry the momentous news to his own Tennessee country and thence down the Mississippi to New Orleans. That the task was undertaken with all due energy is sufficiently attested in a letter written by a Baptist clergyman at Lexington, North Carolina, to a friend, who happened to have been one of Jackson's old teachers at the Waxhaws. "I have to inform you," runs the communication, "that just now the President's express-rider, Bill Phillips, has tore through this little place without stopping. He came and went in a cloud of dust, his horse's tail and his own long hair streaming alike in the wind as they flew by. But as he passed the tavern stand where some were gathered he swung his leather wallet by its straps above his head and shouted — 'Here's the Stuff! Wake up! *War! War with England!!*

THE CREEK WAR 25

War!!!' Then he disappeared in a cloud of dust down the Salisbury Road like a streak of Greased Lightnin'." Nine days brought the indefatigable courier past Hillsboro, Salisbury, Morganton, Jonesboro, and Knoxville to Nashville — a daily average of ninety-five miles over mountains and through uncleared country. In eleven days more the President's dispatches were in the hands of Governor Claiborne at New Orleans.

The joy of the West was unbounded. The frontiersman was always ready for a fight, and just now he especially wanted a fight with England. He resented the insults that his country had suffered at the hands of the English authorities and had little patience with the vacillating policy so long pursued by Congress and the Madison Administration. Other grievances came closer home. For two years the West had been disturbed by Indian wars and intrigues for which the English officers and agents in Canada were held largely responsible. In 1811 Governor Harrison of Indiana Territory defeated the Indians at Tippecanoe. But Tecumseh was even then working among the Creeks, Cherokees, and other southern tribes with a view to a confederation which should be powerful enough to put a stop to the sale of land to the advancing white population. A renewal of the disorders was therefore momentarily expected. Furthermore, the people of the Southwest were as usual on bad terms with their Spanish neighbors in Florida and Texas; they coveted an opportunity for vengeance for wrongs which they had suffered; and some longed for the conquest of Spanish territory. At all events, war with England was the more welcome because Spain, as an ally of that power, was likely to be involved.

Nowhere was the news received with greater enthusiasm than at Nashville; and by no one with more satisfaction than by Andrew Jackson. As major general of militia Jackson had for ten years awaited just such a chance for action. In 1811 he wrote fervently to Harrison offering to come to his assistance in the Wabash expedition with five hundred West Tennesseeans, but his services were not needed. At the close of the year he induced the Governor of his State, William Blount, to inform the War Department that he could have twenty-five hundred men "before Quebec within ninety days" if desired. Again he was refused. But now his opportunity had come. Billy Phillips was hardly on his way to Natchez before Jackson, Blount, and Benton were addressing a mass meeting called to

THE CREEK WAR 27

"ratify" the declaration of war, and on the following day a courier started for Washington with a letter from Jackson tendering the services of twenty-five hundred Tennesseeans and assuring the President, with better patriotism than syntax, that wherever it might please him to find a place of duty for these men he could depend upon them to stay "till they or the last armed foe expires."

After some delay the offer was accepted. Already the fiery major general was dreaming of a conquest of Florida. "You burn with anxiety," ran a proclamation issued to his division in midsummer, "to learn on what theater your arms will find employment. Then turn your eyes to the South! Behold in the province of West Florida a territory whose rivers and harbors are indispensable to the prosperity of the western, and still more so, to the eastern division of our state. . . . It is here that an employment adapted to your situation awaits your courage and your zeal, and while extending in this quarter the boundaries of the Republic to the Gulf of Mexico, you will experience a peculiar satisfaction in having conferred a signal benefit on that section of the Union to which you yourselves immediately belong."

28 THE REIGN OF ANDREW JACKSON

It lay in the cards that Jackson was to be a principal agent in wresting the Florida country from the Spaniards; and while there was at Washington no intention of allowing him to set off posthaste upon the mission, all of the services which he was called upon to render during the war converged directly upon that objective. After what seemed an interminable period of waiting came the first order to move. Fifteen hundred Tennessee troops were to go to New Orleans, ostensibly to protect the city against a possible British attack, but mainly to be quickly available in case an invasion of West Florida should be decided upon; and Jackson, freshly commissioned major general of volunteers, was to lead the expedition.

The rendezvous was fixed at Nashville for early December; and when more than two thousand men, representing almost every family of influence in the western half of the State, presented themselves, Governor Blount authorized the whole number to be mustered. On the 7th of January the hastily equipped detachment started, fourteen hundred infantrymen going down the ice-clogged Cumberland in flatboats and six hundred and seventy mounted riflemen proceeding by land. The Governor sent a letter carrying his blessing. Jackson

THE CREEK WAR 29

responded with an effusive note in which he expressed the hope that "the God of battles may be with us." Parton says with truth that the heart of western Tennessee went down the river with the expedition. In a letter to the Secretary of War Jackson declared that his men had no "constitutional scruples," but would, if so ordered, plant the American eagle on the "walls" of Mobile, Pensacola, and St. Augustine.

After five weeks the troops, in high spirits, reassembled at Natchez. Then came cruel disappointment. From New Orleans Governor James Wilkinson, doubtless moved by hatred of Jackson quite as much as by considerations of public policy, ordered the little army to stay where it was. And on the 15th of March there was placed in the commander's hands a curt note from the Secretary of War saying that the reasons for the undertaking had disappeared, and announcing that the corps under the Tennesseean's command had "ceased to exist."

Jackson flew into a rage — and with more reason than on certain other occasions. He was sure that there was treachery somewhere; at the least, it was all a trick to bring a couple of thousand good Tennessee volunteers within the clutches of

30   THE REIGN OF ANDREW JACKSON

Wilkinson's recruiting officers. He managed to write to the President a temperate letter of protest; but to Governor Blount and to the troops he unbosomed himself with characteristic forcefulness of speech. There was nothing to do but return home. But the irate commander determined to do it in a manner to impress the country. He kept his force intact, drew rations from the commissary department at Natchez, and marched back to Nashville with all the *éclat* that would have attended a returning conqueror. When Wilkinson's subordinates refused to pay the cost of transporting the sick, Jackson pledged his own credit for the purpose, to the amount of twelve thousand dollars. It was on the trying return march that his riflemen conferred on him the happy nickname "Old Hickory."

The Secretary of War later sought to appease the irascible major general by offering a wholly plausible explanation of the sudden reversal of the Government's policy; and the expenses of the troops on the return march were fully met out of the national treasury. But Jackson drew from the experience only gall and wormwood. About the time when the men reached Natchez, Congress definitely authorized the President to take possession of Mobile and that part of Florida west of the

THE CREEK WAR 31

Perdido River; and, back once more in the humdrum life of Nashville, the disappointed officer could only sit idly by while his pet project was successfully carried out by General Wilkinson, the man whom, perhaps above all others, he loathed. But other work was preparing; and, after all, most of Florida was yet to be won.

In the late summer of 1813 the western country was startled by news of a sudden attack of a band of upwards of a thousand Creeks on Fort Mims, Alabama, culminating in a massacre in which two hundred and fifty white men, women, and children lost their lives. It was the most bloody occurrence of the kind in several decades, and it brought instantly to a head a situation which Jackson, in common with many other military men, had long viewed with apprehension.

From time immemorial the broad stretches of hill and valley land southwards from the winding Tennessee to the Gulf were occupied, or used as hunting grounds, by the warlike tribes forming the loose-knit Creek Confederacy. Much of this land was extremely fertile, and most of it required little labor to prepare it for cultivation. Consequently after 1800 the influx of white settlers, mainly cotton raisers, was heavy; and by 1812 the great

32 THE REIGN OF ANDREW JACKSON

triangular area between the Alabama and the Tombigbee, as well as extensive tracts along the upper Tombigbee and the Mobile, was quite fully occupied. The heart of the Creek country was the region about the Coosa and Tallapoosa rivers, which join in central Alabama to form the stream which bears the State's name. But not even this district was immune from encroachment.

The Creeks were not of a sort to submit to the loss of their lands without a struggle. Though Tecumseh, in 1811, had brought them to the point of an uprising, his plans were not carried out, and it remained for the news of hostilities between the United States and Great Britain to rouse the war spirit afresh. In a short time the entire Creek country was aflame. Arms and ammunition the Indians obtained from the Spaniards across the Florida border, and Colonel Edward Nicholls, now stationed at Pensacola as provisional British Governor, gave them open encouragement. The danger was understood not only among the people of the Southwest but in Washington. Before plans of defense could be carried into effect, however, the war broke out, and the wretched people who had crowded into the flimsy stockade called by courtesy Fort Mims were massacred.

THE CREEK WAR

Hardly had the heap of ruins, ghastly with human bodies, ceased to smolder before fleet riders were spreading the news in Georgia, in Louisiana, and in Tennessee. A shudder swept the country. Every exposed community expected to be attacked next. The people's demand for vengeance was overmastering, and from north, west, and east volunteer armies were soon on the march. Tennessee sent two quotas, one from the eastern counties under General John Cocke, the other from the western under Andrew Jackson. When the news of the disaster on the Mobile reached Nashville, Jackson was lying helpless from wounds received in his fight with the Bentons. But he issued the necessary orders from his bed and let it be known with customary vigor that he, the senior major general, and no one else, would lead the expedition; and though three weeks later he started off with his arm tightly bandaged to his side and a shoulder so sore that it could not bear the pressure of an epaulette, lead the expedition he did.

About the middle of October the emaciated but dogged commander brought his forces together, 2700 strong, at Huntsville and began cutting his way across the mountains toward the principal Creek settlements. His plan was to fall suddenly upon these settlements, strike terror into the inhabitants, and force a peace on terms that would guarantee the safety of the frontier populations. Supplies were slow to arrive, and Jackson fumed and stormed. He quarreled desperately, too, with Cocke, whom he unjustly blamed for mismanagement. But at last he was able to emerge on the banks of the Coosa and build a stockade, Fort Strother, to serve as a base for the campaign.

During the months that followed, the intrepid leader was compelled to fight two foes — his insubordinate militiamen and the Creeks. His command consisted partly of militia and partly of volunteers, including many men who had first enlisted for the expedition down the Mississippi. Starvation and disease caused loud murmurings, and after one or two minor victories had been won the militiamen took it into their heads to go back home. Jackson drew up the volunteers across the mutineers' path and drove them back to the camp. Then the volunteers started off, and the militia had to be used to bring them back! At one time the furious general faced a mutinous band single-handed and, swearing that he would shoot the first man who stirred, awed the recalcitrants into obedience. On another occasion he had a youth who

THE CREEK WAR 35

had been guilty of insubordination shot before the whole army as an object lesson. At last it became apparent that nothing could be done with such troops, and the volunteers — such of them as had not already slipped away — were allowed to go home. Governor Blount advised that the whole undertaking be given up. But Jackson wrote him a letter that brought a flush of shame to his cheek, and in a short time fresh forces by the hundreds, with ample supplies, were on the way to Fort Strother. Among the newcomers was a lank, angular-featured frontiersman who answered to the name of Sam Houston.

After having been reduced for a short period to one hundred men, Jackson by early spring had an army of five thousand, including a regiment of regulars, and found it once more possible to act. The enemy decided to make its stand at a spot called by the Indians Tohopeka, by the whites Horseshoe Bend, on the Tallapoosa. Here a thousand warriors, with many women and children, took refuge behind breastworks which they believed impregnable, and here, in late March, Jackson attacked with a force of three thousand men. No quarter was asked and none given, on either side, and the battle quickly became a butchery.

36 THE REIGN OF ANDREW JACKSON

Driven by fire from a thicket of dry brush in which they took refuge, the Creek warriors were shot down or bayoneted by the hundreds; those who plunged into the river for safety were killed as they swam. Scarcely a hundred survived. Among the number was a youth who could speak a little English, and whose broken leg one of the surgeons undertook to treat. Three stalwart riflemen were required to hold the patient. "Lie still, my boy, they will save your life," said Jackson encouragingly, as he came upon the scene. "No good," replied the disconsolate victim. "No good. Cure um now, kill um again!"

The victory practically ended the war. Many of the "Red Sticks," as the Creek braves were called, fled beyond the Florida border; but many — among them the astute half-breed Weathersford, who had ordered the assault on Fort Mims — came in and surrendered. Fort Jackson, built in the river fork, became an outpost of American sovereignty in the very heart of the Creek district. "The fiends of the Tallapoosa," declared the victorious commander in his farewell address to his men, "will no longer murder our women and children, or disturb the quiet of our borders."

Jackson returned to Tennessee to find himself

THE VICTORY OF NEW ORLEANS 37

the most popular man in the State. Nashville gave him the first of what was destined to be a long series of tumultuous receptions; and within a month the news came that William Henry Harrison had resigned his commission and that Jackson had been appointed a major general in the army of the United States, with command in the southwestern district, including Mobile and New Orleans. "Thus did the frontier soldier, who eighteen months earlier had not commanded an expedition or a detachment, come to occupy the highest rank in the army of his country. No other man in that country's service since the Revolution has risen to the top quite so quickly."[1]

By his appointment Jackson became the eventual successor of General Wilkinson, with headquarters at New Orleans. His first move, however, was to pay a visit to Mobile; and on his way thither, in August, 1814, he paused in the Creek country to garner the fruits of his late victory. A council of the surviving chiefs was assembled and a treaty was presented, with a demand that it be signed forthwith. The terms took the Indians aback, but argument was useless. The whites were granted full rights to maintain military posts

[1] Bassett, *The Life of Andrew Jackson*, vol. I, p. 123.

38 THE REIGN OF ANDREW JACKSON

and roads and to navigate the rivers in the Creek lands; the Creeks had to promise to stop trading with British and Spanish posts; and they were made to cede to the United States all the lands which their people had claimed west and southeast of the Coosa River — more than half of their ancient territories. Thus was the glory of the Creek nation brought to an end.

Meanwhile the war with Great Britain was entering a new and threatening phase. No notable successes had been achieved on land, and repeated attempts to reduce Canada had signally failed. On the Great Lakes and the high seas the navy had won glory, but only a handful of privateers was left to keep up the fight. The collapse of Napoleon's power had brought a lull in Europe, and the British were free to concentrate their energies as never before on the conflict in America. The effects were promptly seen in the campaign which led to the capture of Washington and the burning of the Federal Capitol in August, 1814. They were equally manifest in a well-laid plan for a great assault on the country's southern borders and on the great Mississippi Valley beyond.

The last-mentioned project meant that, after two years of immunity, the Southwest had become

THE VICTORY OF NEW ORLEANS 39

a main theater of the war. There was plenty of warning of what was coming, for the British squadron intended for the attack began assembling in the West Indies before the close of summer. No one knew, however, where or when the blow would fall. To Jackson the first necessity seemed to be to make sure of the defenses of Mobile. For a time, at all events, he believed that the attack would be made there, rather than at New Orleans; and an attempt of a British naval force in September to destroy Fort Bowyer, at the entrance to Mobile Bay, confirmed his opinion.

But the chief attraction of Mobile for the General was its proximity to Florida. In July he had written to Washington asking permission to occupy Pensacola. Months passed without a reply. Temptation to action grew; and when, in October, three thousand Tennessee troops arrived under one of the subordinate officers in the recent Creek War, longer hesitation seemed a sign of weakness. Jackson therefore led his forces against the Spanish stronghold, now in British hands, and quickly forced its surrender. His men blew up one of the two forts, and the British blew up the other. Within a week the work was done and the General, well pleased with his exploit, was back at Mobile.

40 THE REIGN OF ANDREW JACKSON

There he found awaiting him, in reply to his July letter, an order from the new Secretary of War, James Monroe, forbidding him to touch Pensacola. No great harm was done, for the invaded territory was no longer neutral soil, and the task of soothing the ruffled feelings of the Spanish court did not prove difficult.

As the autumn wore on, signs multiplied that the first British objective in the South was to be New Orleans, and no efforts were spared by the authorities at Washington to arouse the Southwest to its danger and to stimulate an outpouring of troops sufficient to repel any force that might be landed at the mouth of the Mississippi. On the 21st of November, Jackson set out for the menaced city. Five days later a fleet of fifty vessels, carrying ten thousand veteran British troops under command of Generals Pakenham and Gibbs, started from Jamaica for what was expected to be an easy conquest. On the 10th of December the hostile armada cast anchor off the Louisiana coast. Two weeks later some two thousand redcoats emerged from Lake Borgne, within six or seven miles of New Orleans, when the approach to the city on that side was as yet unguarded by a gun or a man or an entrenchment.

THE VICTORY OF NEW ORLEANS 41

That the "impossible" was now accomplished was due mainly to Jackson, although credit must not be withheld from a dozen energetic subordinate officers nor from the thousands of patriots who made up the rank and file of the hastily gathered forces of defense. Men from Louisiana, Mississippi, Georgia, Kentucky, and Tennessee — all contributed to one of the most remarkable military achievements in our history; although when the fight was over it was found that hundreds were still as unarmed as when they arrived upon the scene.

A preliminary clash, in a dense fog, on the second evening before Christmas served to inspire each army with a wholesome respect for the other. The British decided to postpone further action until their entire force could be brought up, and this gave Jackson just the time he needed to assemble his own scattered divisions, select lines of defense, and throw up breastworks. By the end of the first week of January both sides were ready for the test.

The British army was a splendid body of seven thousand trained soldiers, seamen, and marines.

There were regiments which had helped Wellington to win Talavera, Salamanca, and Victoria, and within a

42 THE REIGN OF ANDREW JACKSON

few short months some of these same regiments were to stand in that thin red line which Ney and Napoleon's guard could never break. Their general, Pakenham, Wellington's brother-in-law, was a distinguished pupil of his illustrious kinsman. Could frontiersmen who had never fought together before, who had never seen the face of a civilized foe, withstand the conquerors of Napoleon? But two branches of the same stubborn race were represented on that little watery plain. The soldiers trained to serve the strongest will in the Old World were face to face with the rough and ready yeomanry embattled for defense by the one man of the new world whose soul had most iron in it. It was Salamanca against Tohopeka, discipline against individual alertness, the Briton of the little Isle against the Briton of the wastes and wilds. But there was one great difference. Wellington, "the Iron Duke," was not there; "Old Hickory" was everywhere along the American lines.[1]

Behind their battery-studded parapets the Americans waited for the British to make an assault. This the invaders did, five thousand strong, on January 8, 1815. The fighting was hard, but the main attack failed at every point. Three British major generals, including Pakenham, were killed early in the action, and the total British loss exceeded two thousand. The American loss was

[1] Brown, *Andrew Jackson*, pp. 75–76.

THE VICTORY OF NEW ORLEANS 43

but seventy-one. The shattered foe fell back, lay inactive for ten days, and then quietly withdrew as they had come. Though Jackson was not noted for piety, he always believed that his success on this occasion was the work of Providence. "Heaven, to be sure," he wrote to Monroe, "has interposed most wonderfully in our behalf, and I am filled with gratitude when I look back to what we have escaped."

By curious irony, the victory had no bearing upon the formal results of the war. A treaty of peace had been signed at Ghent two weeks before, and the news of the pacification and of the exploit at New Orleans reached the distracted President at almost the same time. But who shall say that the battle was not one of the most momentous in American history? It compensated for a score of humiliations suffered by the country in the preceding years. It revived the people's drooping pride and put new energy into the nation's dealings with its rivals, contributing more than any other single event to make this war indeed a "second war of independence." "Now," declared Henry Clay when the news reached him in Paris, "I can go to England without mortification." Finally, the battle brought Andrew

Jackson into his own as the idol and incarnation of the West, and set the western democracy decisively forward as a force to be reckoned with in national affairs.

CHAPTER III

THE "CONQUEST" OF FLORIDA

THE victory at New Orleans made Jackson not only the most popular man in the United States but a figure of international interest. "Napoleon, returning from Elba to eke out the Hundred Days and add the name Waterloo to history, paused now and then a moment to study Jackson at New Orleans. The Duke of Wellington, chosen by assembled Europe to meet the crisis, could find time even at Brussels to call for 'all available information on the abortive expedition against Louisiana.'"[1]

While his countrymen were sounding his praises, the General, however, fell into a controversy with the authorities and people of New Orleans which lent a drab aspect to the closing scene of an otherwise brilliant drama. One of his first acts upon arriving in the defenseless city had been to declare

[1] Buell, *History of Andrew Jackson*, vol. II, pp. 94-95.

martial law; and under the decree the daily life of the inhabitants had been rigorously circumscribed, citizens had been pressed into military service, men under suspicion had been locked up, and large quantities of cotton and other supplies had been seized for the soldiers' use. When Pakenham's army was defeated, people expected an immediate return to normal conditions. Jackson, however, proposed to take no chances. Neither the sailing of the British fleet nor the receipt of the news of peace from Admiral Cochrane influenced him to relax his vigilance, and only after official instructions came from Washington in the middle of March was the ban lifted.

Meanwhile a violent quarrel had broken out between the commander and the civil authorities, who naturally wished to resume their accustomed functions. Finding that the Creoles were systematically evading service by registering as French citizens, Jackson abruptly ordered all such people from the city; and he was responsible for numerous other arbitrary acts. Protests were lodged, and some people threatened judicial proceedings. But they might have saved their breath. Jackson was not the man to argue matters of the kind. A leading Creole who published an especially pointed

THE "CONQUEST" OF FLORIDA 47

protest was clapped into prison, and when the Federal district judge, Hall, issued a writ of *habeas corpus* in his behalf, Jackson had him also shut up.

As soon as he was liberated, the irate judge summoned Jackson into court to show why he should not be held in contempt. Beyond a blanket vindication of his acts, the General would not plead. "I will not answer interrogatories," he declared. "I may have erred, but my motives cannot be misinterpreted." The judge thereupon imposed a fine of one thousand dollars, the only question being, he declared, "whether the Law should bend to the General or the General to the Law." Jackson accepted the sentence with equanimity, and to a group of admirers who drew him in a carriage from the court room to one of the leading coffeehouses, he expressed lofty sentiments on the obligation of citizens of every rank to obey the laws and uphold the courts. Twenty-nine years afterwards Congress voted reimbursement to the full amount of the fine with interest.

For three weeks after the arrival of the treaty of peace Jackson lingered at New Orleans, haggling by day with the contractors and merchants whose cotton, blankets, and bacon were yet to be paid for, and enjoying in the evening the festivities planned in his honor by grateful citizens. His pleasure in the gala affairs of the time was doubled by the presence of his wife, who one day arrived quite unexpectedly in the company of some Tennessee friends. Mrs. Jackson was a typical frontier planter's wife — kind-hearted, sincere, benevolent, thrifty, pious, but unlettered and wholly innocent of polished manners. In all her forty-eight years she had never seen a city more pretentious than Nashville. She was, moreover, stout and florid, and it may be supposed that in her rustic garb she was a somewhat conspicuous figure among the fashionable ladies of New Orleans society.

But the wife of Jackson's accomplished friend and future Secretary of State, Edward Livingston, fitted her out with fashionable clothes and tactfully instructed her in the niceties of etiquette, and ere long she was able to demean herself, if not without a betrayal of her unfamiliarity with the environment, at all events to the complete satisfaction of the General. The latter's devotion to his wife was a matter of much comment. "Debonair as he had been in his association with the Creole belles, he never missed an opportunity to demonstrate that he considered the short, stout, beaming matron at his side the perfection of her sex and far

THE "CONQUEST" OF FLORIDA 49

and away the most charming woman in the world."[1] "Aunt Rachel," as she was known throughout western Tennessee, lived to see the hero of New Orleans elected President, but not to share with him the honors of the position. "I have sometimes thought," said Thomas Hart Benton, "that General Jackson might have been a more equable tenant of the White House than he was had she been spared to share it with him. At all events, she was the only human being on earth who ever possessed the power to swerve his mighty will or soothe his fierce temper."

Shortly before their departure the Jacksons were guests of honor at a grand ball at the Academy. The upper floor was arranged for dancing and the lower for supper, and the entire building was aglow with flowers, colored lamps, and transparencies. As the evening wore on and the dances of polite society had their due turn, the General finally avowed that he and his bonny wife would show the proud city folk what *real* dancing was. A somewhat cynical observer — a certain Nolte, whom Jackson had just forced to his own terms in a settlement for war supplies — records his impression as follows: "After supper we were treated to

[1] Buell, *History of Andrew Jackson*, vol. II, p. 97.

50 THE REIGN OF ANDREW JACKSON

a most delicious *pas de deux* by the conqueror and his spouse. To see these two figures, the General, a long haggard man, with limbs like a skeleton, and Madame la Générale, a short fat dumpling, bobbing opposite each other like half-drunken Indians, to the wild melody of *Possum up de Gum Tree*, and endeavoring to make a spring into the air, was very remarkable, and far more edifying a spectacle than any European ballet could possibly have furnished." But Jackson was only less proud of his accomplishments as a dancer than as a fighter, and it was the part of discretion for a man of Nolte's critical turn to keep a straight face on this occasion.

In early April the General and his wife started homeward, the latter bearing as a parting gift from the women of New Orleans the somewhat gaudy set of topaz jewelry which she wears in her most familiar portrait. The trip was a continuous ovation, and at Nashville a series of festivities wound up with a banquet attended by the most distinguished soldiers and citizens of Tennessee and presided over by the Governor of the State. Other cities gave dinners, and legislatures voted swords and addresses. A period of rest at the Hermitage was interrupted in the autumn of 1815 by a horseback trip to Washington which involved a

THE "CONQUEST" OF FLORIDA 51

succession of dinners and receptions. But after a few months the much fêted soldier was back at Nashville, ready, as he said, to "resume the cultivation of that friendly intercourse with my friends and neighbors which has heretofore constituted so great a portion of my happiness."

After Jackson had talked over his actions at New Orleans with both the President and the Secretary of War, he had received, as he says, "a chart blank," approving his "whole proceedings"; so he had nothing further to worry about on that score. The national army had been reorganized on a peace footing, in two divisions, each under command of a major general. The northern division fell to Jacob Brown of New York, the hero of Lundy's Lane; the southern fell to Jackson, with headquarters at Nashville.

Jackson was the last man to suppose that warfare in the southern half of the United States was a thing of the past. He knew that the late contest had left the southern Indians restless and that the existing treaties were likely to be repudiated at any moment. Florida was still in the hands of the Spaniards, and he had never a doubt that some day this territory would have to be conquered and annexed. Moreover Jackson believed for some years after 1815, according to General Eaton, that Great Britain would again make war on the United States, using Florida as a base. At all events, it can have caused the General no surprise — or regret — to be called again into active service on the Florida border before the close of 1817.

The hold of the Spaniards upon Florida had been so far weakened by the War of 1812 that after the restoration of peace they occupied only three important points — Pensacola, St. Marks, and St. Augustine. The rest of the territory became a No Man's Land, an ideal resort for desperate adventurers of every race and description. There was a considerable Indian population, consisting mainly of Seminoles, a tribe belonging to the Creek Confederacy, together with other Creeks who had fled across the border to escape the vengeance of Jackson at Tohopeka. All were bitterly hostile to the United States. There were Spanish freebooters, Irish roustabouts, Scotch free lances, and runaway slaves — a nondescript lot, and all ready for any undertaking that promised excitement, revenge, or booty. Furthermore there were some British soldiers who had remained on their own responsibility after the troops were withdrawn. The leading spirit among these was

THE "CONQUEST" OF FLORIDA 53

Colonel Edward Nicholls, who had already made himself obnoxious to the United States by his conduct at Pensacola.

At the close of the war Nicholls and his men built a fort on the Apalachicola, fifteen miles from the Gulf, and began again to collect and organize fugitive slaves, Indians, and adventurers of every sort, whom they employed on raids into the territory of the United States and in attacks upon its inhabitants. The Creeks were falsely informed that in the Treaty of Ghent the United States had promised to give up all lands taken from them during the late war, and they were thus incited to rise in vindication of their alleged rights. What Nicholls was aiming at came out when, in company with several chieftains, he returned to England to ask for an alliance between the "mother country" and his buccaneer state. He met no encouragement, however, and in reply to an American protest the British Government repudiated his acts. His rôle was nevertheless promptly taken up by a misguided Scotch trader, Alexander Arbuthnot, and the reign of lawlessness continued.

After all, it was Spain's business to keep order on the frontier; and the United States waited a year and a half for the Madrid Government to give evidence of intent to do so. But, as nothing but vain promises were forthcoming, some American troops engaged in building a fort on the Apalachicola, just north of the boundary line, marched down the river in July, 1816, bombarded Nicholls's Negro Fort, blew up its magazine, and practically exterminated the negro and Indian garrison. A menace to the slave property of southern Georgia was thus removed, but the bigger problem remained. The Seminoles were restive; the refugee Creeks kept up their forays across the border; and the rich lands acquired by the Treaty of Fort Jackson were fast filling with white settlers who clamored for protection. Though the Monroe Administration had opened negotiations for the cession of the whole Florida country to the United States, progress was slow and the outcome doubtful.

Matters came to a head in the closing weeks of 1817. General Gaines, who was in command on the Florida border, had tried repeatedly to get an interview with the principal "Red Stick" chieftain, but all of his overtures had been repulsed. Finally he sent a detachment of soldiers to conduct the dignitary and his warriors from their village at Fowltown, on the American side of the line, to a designated parley ground. In no mood for nego-

THE "CONQUEST" OF FLORIDA 55

tiation, the chief ordered his followers to fire on the visitors; whereupon the latter seized and destroyed the village.

The fight at Fowltown may be regarded as the beginning of the Seminole War. General Gaines was directed to begin operations against the Indians and to pursue them if necessary into East Florida; but before he could carry out his orders, Jackson was put in personal command of the forces acting against the Indians and was instructed to concentrate all of the troops in his department at Fort Scott and to obtain from the Governors of Georgia and Tennessee such other assistance as he should need.

Jackson received his orders at the Hermitage. Governor Blount was absent from Nashville, but the eager commander went ahead raising troops on his own responsibility. Nothing was so certain to whet his appetite for action as the prospect of a war in Florida. Not only did his instructions authorize him to pursue the enemy, under certain conditions, into Spanish territory, but from the first he himself conceived of the enterprise as decidedly more than a punitive expedition. The United States wanted Florida and was at the moment trying to induce Spain to give it up.

56 THE REIGN OF ANDREW JACKSON

Here was the chance to take it regardless of Spain. "Let it be signified to me through any channel (say Mr. J. Rhea)," wrote the Major General to the President, "that the possession of the Floridas would be desirable to the United States, and in sixty days it will be accomplished."

This "Rhea letter" became the innocent source of one of the most famous controversies in American history. Jackson supposed that the communication had been promptly delivered to Monroe, and that his plan for the conquest of Florida had the full, if secret, approval of the Administration. Instructions from the Secretary of War, Calhoun, seemed susceptible of no other interpretation; besides, the conqueror subsequently maintained that he received through Rhea the assurance that he coveted. Monroe, however, later denied flatly that he had given any orders of the kind. Indeed he said that through a peculiar combination of circumstances he had not even read Jackson's letter until long after the Florida campaign was ended. Each man, no doubt, thought he was telling the truth, and historians will probably always differ upon the merits of the case. The one thing that is perfectly certain is that Jackson, when he carried his troops into Florida in 1818, believed that the

THE "CONQUEST" OF FLORIDA   57

Government expected him to prepare the territory for permanent American occupation.

In early March, Jackson was at Fort Scott, on the Georgia frontier, with about two thousand men. Though he expected other forces, Jackson found that scarcity of rations made it inadvisable to wait for them, and he therefore marched his army on as rapidly as possible down the soggy bank of the Apalachicola, past the ruins of Negro Fort, into Florida, where he found in readiness the provisions which had been sent forward by way of Mobile. Turning eastward, Jackson bore down upon the Spanish settlement of St. Marks, where it was rumored that the hostile natives had assembled in considerable numbers. A small fleet of gunboats from Mobile and New Orleans was ordered to move along the coast and intercept any fugitives, "white, red, or black." Upwards of two thousand friendly Indians joined the land expedition, and the invasion became from a military standpoint a sheer farce. The Seminoles were utterly unprepared for war, and their villages were taken possession of, one by one, without opposition. At St. Marks the Indians fled precipitately, and the little Spanish garrison, after a glimpse of the investing force, asked only that receipts be

58 THE REIGN OF ANDREW JACKSON

given for the movable property confiscated. The Seminole War was over almost before it was begun.

But Jackson was not in Florida simply to quell the Seminoles. He was there to vindicate the honor and establish the sovereignty of the United States. Hence there was further work for him to do. The British instigators of lawlessness were to be apprehended; the surviving evidences of Spanish authority were to be obliterated. Both objects Jackson attained with characteristic speed and thoroughness. At St. Marks he made Arbuthnot a prisoner; at Suwanee he captured another meddler by the name of Ambrister; and after a court-martial he hanged one and shot the other in the presence of the chieftains whom these men had deceived into thinking that Great Britain stood ready to come to the red man's relief. Two Indian chiefs who were considered ringleaders he likewise executed. Then, leaving St. Marks in the possession of two hundred troops, Jackson advanced upon Pensacola, the main seat of Spanish authority in the colony.

From the Governor, Don José Callava, now came a dignified note of protest; but the invader's only reply was an announcement of his purpose to take possession of the town, on the ground that its

THE "CONQUEST" OF FLORIDA 59

population had encouraged the Indians and given them supplies. On May 24, 1818, the American forces and their allies marched in, unopposed, and the commander coolly apprised Callava that he would "assume the government until the transaction can be amicably adjusted by the two governments." "If, contrary to my hopes," responded the Spanish dignitary, "Your Excellency should persist in your intention to occupy this fortress, which I am resolved to defend to the last extremity, I shall repel force by force; and he who resists aggression can never be considered an aggressor. God preserve Your Excellency many years." To which Jackson replied that "resistance would be a wanton sacrifice of blood," and that he could not but remark on the Governor's inconsistency in presuming himself capable of repelling an army which had conquered Indian tribes admittedly too powerful for the Spaniards to control.

When the Americans approached the fort in which Callava had taken refuge, they were received with a volley which they answered, as Jackson tells us, with "a nine-pound piece and five eight-inch howitzers." The Spaniards, whose only purpose was to make a decent show of defending the place, then ran up the white flag and were allowed to march out with the honors of war. The victor sent the Governor and soldiery off to Havana, installed a United States collector of customs, stationed a United States garrison in the fort, and on the following day set out on his way to Tennessee.

In a five months' campaign Jackson had established peace on the border, had broken the power of the hostile Indians, and had substantially conquered Florida. Not a white man in his army had been killed in battle, and not even the most extravagant eulogist could aver that the war had been a great military triumph. None the less, the people — especially in the West and South — were intensely pleased. Life in the frontier regions would now be safer; and the acquisition of the coveted Florida country was brought appreciably nearer. The popular sentiment on the latter subject found characteristic expression in a toast at a banquet given at Nashville in honor of the returning conqueror: "Pensacola — Spanish perfidy and Indian barbarity rendered its capture necessary. May our Government never surrender it from the fear of war!"

It was easy enough for Jackson to "take" Florida and for the people to rejoice in the exploit. To defend or explain away the irregular features

THE "CONQUEST" OF FLORIDA 61

of the act was, however, quite a different matter; and that was the task which fell to the authorities at Washington. "The territory of a friendly power had been invaded, its officers deposed, its towns and fortresses taken possession of; two citizens of another friendly and powerful nation had been executed in scandalously summary fashion, upon suspicion rather than evidence." The Spanish Minister, Onis, wrathfully protested to the Secretary of State and demanded that Jackson be punished; while from London Rush quoted Castlereagh as saying that English feeling was so wrought up that war could be produced by the raising of a finger.

Monroe and his Cabinet were therefore given many anxious days and sleepless nights. They wanted to buy Florida, not conquer it. They had entertained no thought of authorizing the things that Jackson had done. They recognized that the Tennesseean's crude notions of international law could not be upheld in dealings with proud European States. Yet it was borne in upon them from every side that the nation approved what had been done; and the politically ambitious might well think twice before casting any slur upon the acts of the people's hero. Moreover the irascibility of the conqueror himself was known and feared. Calhoun, the Secretary of War, who was specially annoyed because his instructions had not been followed, favored a public censure. On the other hand, John Quincy Adams, the Secretary of State, took the ground that everything that Jackson had done was "defensive and incident to his main duty to crush the Seminoles." The Administration finally reached the decision to surrender the posts but otherwise to back up the General, in the hope of convincing Spain of the futility of trying longer to hold Florida. Monroe explained the necessities of the situation to Jackson as tactfully as he could, leaving him under the impression — which was corrected only in 1830 — that Crawford, rather than Calhoun, was the member of the Cabinet who had held out against him.

But the controversy spread beyond the Cabinet circle. During the winter of 1818-19 Congress took it up, and a determined effort was made to carry a vote of censure. The debate in the House — with galleries crowded to suffocation, we are informed by the *National Intelligencer* — lasted four weeks and was notable for bringing Clay for the first time publicly into opposition to the Tennesseean. The resolutions containing the censure

THE "CONQUEST" OF FLORIDA 63

were voted down, however, by a majority of almost two to one. In the Senate a select committee, after a laborious investigation, brought in an unfavorable report, but no further action was taken.

When the discussion in Congress was at its height, Jackson himself appeared in Washington. Certain friends at the capital, fearing that his outbursts of temper would prejudice his case, urged him to remain at home, but others assured him that his presence was needed. To his neighbor, Major Lewis, Jackson confided: "A lot of d —— d rascals, with Clay at their head — and maybe with Adams in the rear-guard — are setting up a conspiracy against me. I'm going there to see it out with them."

Until vindicated by the House vote, he remained quietly in his hotel. After that he felt free to pay and receive calls, attend dinners, and accept the tokens of regard which were showered upon him. It was now that he paid his first visit to a number of the larger eastern cities. Philadelphia fêted him four days. In New York the freedom of the city was presented by the mayor on a delicately inscribed parchment enclosed in a gold box, and Tammany gave a great dinner at which the leading guest, to the dismay of the young Van Buren and other supporters of Crawford, toasted DeWitt Clinton, the leader of the opposing Republican faction. At Baltimore there was a dinner, and the city council asked the visitor to sit for a picture by Peale for the adornment of the council room. Here the General was handed a copy of the Senate committee's report, abounding in strictures on his Seminole campaign. Hastening back to Washington, he filled the air with threats, and was narrowly prevented from personally assaulting a member of the investigating committee. When, however, it appeared that the report was to be allowed to repose for all time on the table, Jackson's indignation cooled, and soon he was on his way back to Tennessee. With him went the news that Adams and Onis had signed a treaty of "amity, settlements, and limits," whereby for a consideration of five million dollars the sovereignty of all Florida was transferred to the United States. This treaty, as Jackson viewed it, was the crowning vindication of the acts which had been called in question; and public sentiment agreed with him.

Dilatory tactics on the part of the Madrid Government delayed the actual transfer of the territory more than two years. After having twice refused, Jackson at length accepted the governorship of

THE "CONQUEST" OF FLORIDA 65

Florida, and in the early summer of 1821 he set out, by way of New Orleans, for his new post. Mrs. Jackson went with him, although she had no liking for either the territory or its people. On the morning of the 17th of July the formal transfer took place. A procession was formed, consisting of such American soldiers as were on the spot. A ship's band briskly played *The Star Spangled Banner* and the new Governor rode proudly at the fore as the procession moved along Main Street to the government house, where ex-Governor Callava with his staff was in waiting. The Spanish flag was hauled down, the American was run up, the keys were handed over, and the remaining members of the garrison were sent off to the vessels which on the morrow were to bear them on their way to Cuba. Only Callava and a few other officials and merchants stayed behind to close up matters of public and private business.

Jackson's governorship was brief and stormy. In the first place, he had no taste for administrative routine, and he found no such opportunity as he had hoped for to confer favors upon his friends. "I am sure our stay here will not be long," wrote Mrs. Jackson to a brother in early August. "This office does not suit my husband. . . .

There never was a man more disappointed than he has been. He has not the power to appoint one of his friends." In the second place, the new Governor's status was wholly anomalous, since Congress had extended to the territory only the revenue and anti-slave-trade laws, leaving Jackson to exercise in other matters the rather vague powers of the captain general of Cuba and of the Spanish governors of the Floridas. And in the third place, before his first twenty-four hours were up, the new executive fell into a desperate quarrel with his predecessor, a man of sufficiently similar temperament to make the contest a source of sport for the gods.

Jackson was prepared to believe the worst of any Spaniard, and his relations with Callava grew steadily more strained until finally, with a view to obtaining possession of certain deeds and other legal papers, he had the irate dignitary shut up overnight in the calaboose. Then he fell upon the judge of the Western District of Florida for issuing a writ of *habeas corpus* in the Spaniard's behalf; and all parties — Jackson, Callava, and the judge — swamped the wearied officials at Washington with "statements" and "exhibitions" setting forth in lurid phraseology their respective views upon the questions involved. Callava finally carried his complaints to the capital in person and stirred the Spanish Minister to a fresh bombardment of the White House. Monroe's Cabinet spent three days discussing the subject, without coming to a decision. Many were in honest doubt as to the principles of law involved; some were fearful of the political effects of any stand they might take; all were inexpressibly relieved when, late in the year, word came that "Don Andrew Jackson" had resigned the governorship and was proposing to retire to private life at the Hermitage.

CHAPTER IV

THE DEATH OF "KING CAUCUS"

ON a bracing November afternoon in 1821 Jackson rode up with his family to the Hermitage free for the first time in thirty-two years from all responsibility of civil and military office. He was now fifty-four years old and much broken by exposure and disease; the prospect of spending the remainder of his days among his hospitable neighbors on the banks of the Cumberland yielded deep satisfaction. The home-loving Mrs. Jackson, too, earnestly desired that he should not again be drawn into the swirl of public life. "I do hope," she wrote plaintively to a niece soon after her return to the Hermitage, "they will leave Mr. Jackson alone. He is not a well man and never will be unless they allow him to rest. He has done his share for the country. How little time has he had to himself or for his own interests in the thirty years of our wedded life. In all that time he has not spent one-fourth of his

THE DEATH OF "KING CAUCUS" 69

days under his own roof. The rest of the time away, traveling, holding court, or at the capital of the country, or in camp, or fighting its battles, or treating with the Indians; mercy knows what not."

The intent to retire was honest enough but not so easy to carry out. The conqueror of the Creeks and Seminoles belonged not merely to Tennessee but to the entire Southwest; the victor of New Orleans belonged to the Nation. Already there was talk — "talk everlastingly," Mrs. Jackson tells us in the letter just quoted — of making the hero President. Jackson, furthermore, was not the type of man to sit idly by while great scenes were enacted on the political stage. When he returned from Florida, he faced the future with the weary vision of a sick man. Rest and reviving strength, however, put the old vim into his words and acts. In two years he was a second time taking a seat in the United States Senate, in three he was contesting for the presidency, and in seven he was moving into the White House.

The glimpses which one gets of the General's surroundings and habits during his brief interval of repose create a pleasing impression. Following the winding turnpike westward from Nashville a distance of nine or ten miles and rumbling across the old wooden bridge over Stone River, a visitor would find himself at Hermitage Farm. The estate contained at that time somewhat more than a thousand acres, of which four hundred were under cultivation and the remainder luxuriant forest. Negro cabins stood here and there, and in one corner was a little brick church which the proprietor had built for the solace of his wife. In the center of a well-kept lawn, flanked with cedars and oaks, stood the family mansion, the Hermitage, whose construction had been begun at the close of the Seminole War in 1819. The building was of brick, two stories high, with a double wooden piazza in both front and rear. The rooms were small and simply furnished, the chief adornment being portraits of the General and his friends, though later was added the familiar painting of Mrs. Jackson. Lavasseur, who as private secretary of La Fayette visited the place in 1825, was greatly surprised to find a person of Jackson's renown living in a structure which in France would hardly suffice for the porter's lodge at the château of a man of similar standing. But western Tennessee afforded nothing finer, and Jackson considered himself palatially housed.

Life on the Hermitage estate had its full share

THE DEATH OF "KING CAUCUS" 71

of the charm of the old South. After breakfasting at eight or nine, the proprietor spent the day riding over his broad acres, giving instructions to his workmen, keeping up his accounts, chatting with neighbors and passers-by, and devouring the newspapers with a zeal born of unremitting interest in public affairs. After the evening meal the family gathered on the cool piazza in summer, or around the blazing hearth of the great living room in winter, and spent the hours until the early bedtime in telling stories, discussing local and national happenings, or listening to the news of distant localities as retailed by the casual visitor. The hospitality of the Jackson home was proverbial. The General's army friends came often to see him. Political leaders and advisers flocked to the place. Clergymen of all denominations were received with special warmth by Mrs. Jackson. Eastern men of distinction, when traveling to the West, came to pay their respects. No foreigner who penetrated as far as the Mississippi Valley would think of returning to his native land without calling upon the picturesque figure at the Hermitage.

Chief among visitors from abroad was La Fayette. The two men met in Washington in 1824 and formed an instant attachment for each other.

72 THE REIGN OF ANDREW JACKSON

The great French patriot was greeted at Nashville the following year with a public reception and banquet at which Jackson, as the first citizen of the State, did the honors. Afterwards he spent some days in the Jackson home, and one can imagine the avidity with which the two men discussed the American and French revolutions, Napoleon, and the late New Orleans campaign.

Jackson was first and last a democrat. He never lost touch with the commonest people. Nevertheless there was always something of the grand manner about him. On formal and ceremonial occasions he bore himself with becoming dignity and even grace; in dress he was, as a rule, punctilious. During his years at the Hermitage he was accustomed to ride about in a carriage drawn by four spirited iron-gray horses, attended by servants in blue livery with brass buttons, glazed hats, and silver bands. "A very big man, sir," declared an old hotel waiter to the visiting biographer Parton long afterwards. "We had many big men, sir, in Nashville at that time, but General Jackson was the biggest man of them all. I knew the General, sir; but he always had so many people around him when he came to town that it was not often I could get a chance to say anything to him."

THE DEATH OF "KING CAUCUS" 73

The question as to who first proposed Jackson for the presidency will probably never be answered. The victory at New Orleans evidently brought the idea into many minds. As the campaign of 1816 was beginning, Aaron Burr wrote to his son-in-law that, if the country wanted a President of firmness and decision, "that man is Andrew Jackson." Not apparently until 1821 was the suggestion put forward in such a way as to lead Jackson himself to take note of it. Even then he scoffed at it. To a friend who assured him that he was not "safe from the presidency" in 1824, he replied: "I really hope you don't think that I am d —— fool enough to believe that. No sir; I may be pretty well satisfied with myself in some things, but am not vain enough for that." On another occasion he declared: "No sir; I know what I am fit for. I can command a body of men in a rough way; but I am not fit to be President."

It really mattered little what the General himself thought. His Tennessee friends had conceived the idea that he could be elected, and already they were at work to realize this vision. One of the most active was John H. Eaton, who had lately written the hero's biography down to the return from New Orleans. Another of his friends was

74 THE REIGN OF ANDREW JACKSON

Governor Blount. John Rhea, Felix Grundy, and half a dozen more helped. But the man who really made Jackson President was his near neighbor and his inseparable companion of later years, William B. Lewis.

In a day of astute politicians Major Lewis was one of the cleverest. He knew Jackson more intimately than did any other man and could sway him readily to his purposes in all matters upon which the General's mind was not absolutely made up. He had a wide acquaintance over the country; he was possessed of ample means and leisure; he was an adept at pulling judiciously laid and well-concealed political wires; he fully understood the ideas, aspirations, and feelings of the classes whose support was necessary to the success of his plans. In the present juncture he worked on two main lines: first, to arouse Jackson's own State to a feverish enthusiasm for the candidacy of its "favorite son," and, second, to start apparently spontaneous Jackson movements in various sections of the country, in such a manner that their cumulative effect would be to create an impression of a nation-wide and irresistible demand for the victor of New Orleans as a candidate.

Tennessee was easily stirred. That the General

THE DEATH OF "KING CAUCUS" 75

merited the highest honor within the gift of the people required no argument among his fellow citizens. The first open steps were taken in January, 1822, when the *Gazette* and other Nashville papers sounded the clarion call. The response was overwhelming; and when Jackson himself, in reply to a letter from Grundy, diplomatically declared that he would "neither seek nor shun" the presidency, his candidacy was regarded as an established fact. On the 20th of July, the Legislature of the State placed him formally in nomination. Meanwhile Lewis had gone to North Carolina to work up sentiment there, and by the close of the year assurances of support were coming in satisfactorily. From being skeptical or at best indifferent, Jackson himself had come to share the enthusiasm of his assiduous friends.

The Jackson managers banked from the first upon two main assets: one was the exceptional popularity of their candidate, especially in the South and West; the other was a political situation so muddled that at the coming election it might be made to yield almost any result. For upwards of a generation the presidency and vice presidency had been at the disposal of a working alliance of Virginia and New York, buttressed by such support

76 THE REIGN OF ANDREW JACKSON

as was needed from other controllable States. Virginia regularly got the presidency, New York (except at the time of the Clinton defection of 1812) the vice presidency. After the second election of Monroe, in 1820, however, there were multiplying signs that this affiliation of interests had reached the end of its tether. In the first place, the Virginia dynasty had run out; at all events Virginia had no candidate to offer and was preparing to turn its support to a Georgian of Virginian birth, William H. Crawford. In the second place, party lines had totally disappeared, and the unifying and stabilizing influences of party names and affiliations could not be counted on to keep down the number of independent candidacies. Already, indeed, by the end of 1822 there were a half-dozen avowed candidates, three of whom had seats at Monroe's Cabinet table. Each was the representative of a section or of a distinct interest, rather than of a party, and no one was likely to feel under any compulsion to withdraw from the race at a preliminary stage.

New England offered John Quincy Adams. She did so with reluctance, for the old Federalist elements had never forgiven him for his desertion to the Republican camp in the days of the embargo,

THE DEATH OF "KING CAUCUS" 77

while the back country democracy had always looked upon him as an alien. But he was the section's only available man — indeed, the only promising candidate from any Northern State. His frigid manner was against him. But he had had a long and honorable diplomatic career; he was winning new distinction as Secretary of State; and he could expect to profit both by the feeling that the North was entitled to the presidency and by the fact that he was the only candidate from a non-slave State.

Crawford, Secretary of the Treasury, was the heir apparent of the Virginia dynasty. Formerly this would have meant a clear road to the White House. Even now it was supposed to be a tremendous asset; and notwithstanding the Georgian's personal unpopularity in most parts of the country, his advantages as the "regular candidate," coupled with the long and careful campaign carried on in his behalf, were expected by many keen observers to pull him through.

A third candidate within the Cabinet circle was Calhoun, Secretary of War. Like Crawford, he could expect to reach the presidency only by winning the support of one or more of the greater Northern States. For a while he had hopes of Pennsylvania. When it appeared that he had nothing to look for in this direction, he resigned himself to the conclusion that, since he was yet hardly forty years of age, his time had not yet come.

For the first time, the West now put forward candidates — two of them, Clay and Jackson. Clay was a Kentuckian, of Virginian birth and breeding, in whom were mingled the leading characteristics of both his native and his adopted section. He was "impetuous, wilful, high-spirited, daring, jealous, but, withal, a lovable man." For a decade he had been the most conspicuous figure in the national House of Representatives. He had raised the speakership to a high level of importance and through its power had fashioned a set of issues, reflective of western and middle-state ideas, upon which the politics of the country turned for more than a quarter of a century. As befitted a "great conciliator," he had admirers in every corner of the land. Whether his strength could be sufficiently massed to yield electoral results remained to be discovered.

But what of Jackson? If, as one writer has said, Clay was one of the favorites of the West, Jackson was the West itself. "While Clay was able to

THE DEATH OF "KING CAUCUS" 79

voice, with statesmanlike ability, the demand for economic legislation to promote her interests, and while he exercised an extraordinary fascination by his personal magnetism and his eloquence, he never became the hero of the great masses of the West; he appealed rather to the more intelligent — to the men of business and of property."[1] Jackson, however, was the very personification of the contentious, self-confident, nationalistic democracy of the interior. He could make no claim to statesmanship. He had held no important legislative or administrative position in his State, and his brief career in Congress was entirely without distinction. He was a man of action, not a theorist, and his views on public questions were, even as late as 1820, not clear cut or widely known. In a general way he represented the school of Randolph and Monroe, rather than that of Jefferson and Madison. He was a moderate protectionist, because he believed that domestic manufactures would make the United States independent of European countries in time of war. On the Bank and internal improvements his mind was not made up, although he was inclined to regard both as unconstitutional.

Jackson's attitude toward the leading political

[1] Turner, *Rise of the New West*, p. 188.

80 THE REIGN OF ANDREW JACKSON

personalities of the time left no room for doubt. He supported Monroe in 1816 and in 1820 and continued on friendly terms with him notwithstanding the President's failure on certain occasions to follow his advice. Among the new contenders for the presidency the one he disliked most was Crawford. "As to Wm. H. Crawford," he wrote to a friend in 1821, "you know my opinion. I would support the Devil first." Clay, also, he disliked — partly out of recollection of the Kentuckian's censorious attitude during the Seminole debates, partly because of the natural rivalry between the two men for the favor of the western people. Clay fully reciprocated by refusing to believe that "killing 2500 Englishmen at New Orleans" qualified Jackson for the "various difficult and complicated duties of the chief magistracy." Toward Adams, Jackson was not ill disposed; before he decided to permit his own name to be used, he said that he would give his support in 1824 to the New Englander — unless one other person should be brought forward. That person was Calhoun, for whom, among all the candidates of the day, he thus far had the warmest regard.

Among so many aspirants — and not all have been mentioned — how should the people make up

THE DEATH OF "KING CAUCUS" 81

their minds? In earlier days the party caucuses in Congress would have eliminated various candidates, and the voters would have found themselves called upon to make a choice between probably but two opponents. The caucus was an informal, voluntary gathering of the party members in the two houses to canvass the political situation and decide upon the men to be supported by the rank and file of the party for the presidency and vice presidency. In the lack of other nominating machinery it served a useful purpose, and nominations had been commonly made in this manner from 1796 onwards. There were obvious objections to the plan — chiefly that the authority exercised was assumed rather than delegated — and, as the campaign of 1824 approached, opposition flared up in a very impressive manner.

Crawford, as the "regular" candidate, wanted a caucus, and his adherents supported him in the wish. But all his rivals were opposed to it, partly because they felt that they could not gain a caucus nomination, partly because their followers generally objected to the system. "King Caucus" became the target of general criticism. Newspapers, except those for Crawford, denounced the old system; legislatures passed resolutions against it; public meetings condemned it; ponderous pamphlets were hurled at it; the campaigns of Jackson and Clay, in particular, found their keynote in hostility toward it. Failing to perceive that under the changed circumstances a caucus nomination might become a liability rather than an asset, the Crawford element pushed its plans, and on February 14, 1824, a caucus — destined to be the last of the kind in the country — was duly held. It proved a fiasco, for it was attended by only sixty-six persons. Crawford was "recommended to the people of the United States" by an almost unanimous vote, but the only effect was to infuse fresh energy into the campaigns of his leading competitors. "The caucus," wrote Daniel Webster to his brother Ezekiel, "has hurt nobody but its friends."

For the first time in eight years the country witnessed a real presidential contest. The campaign, none the less, was one in which the candidates themselves took but little active part. The days of "swinging around the circle" had not yet dawned in our national politics, nor had even those of the "front-porch" campaign. Adams made no effort either to be nominated or to be elected, retaining throughout the contest that austere reserve

THE DEATH OF "KING CAUCUS" 83

in public manner which contrasted so singularly with his amiability and good humor in private life. Jackson remained quietly at the Hermitage, replying to correspondents and acknowledging expressions of support, but leaving to his managers the work of winning the voters. Clay, whose oratorical gifts would have made him an invincible twentieth century campaigner, contented himself with a few interviews and speeches. The candidate who normally would have taken most active personal part in the campaign was Crawford. But in August, 1823 — six months before the caucus nomination — he was stricken with paralysis and rendered speechless, almost blind, and practically helpless. For months he hovered between life and death in a "mansion" on the outskirts of Washington, while his friends labored to conceal the seriousness of his condition and to keep his canvass going. Gradually he rallied; but his powerful frame was shattered, and even when the caucus discharged its appointed task of nominating him, the politicians were cold-heartedly speculating upon who would receive the "old republican" support if he should die. He recovered and lived ten years; but his chances of the presidency were much diminished by his ill fortune. "He had fallen with his face toward the goal, with his eyes and his heart fixed upon it."

As the canvass progressed, Jackson steadily gained. His election to the United States Senate, in the autumn of 1823, over a stanch supporter of Crawford showed that his own State was acting in good faith when it proposed him for the higher position. Clever propaganda turned Pennsylvania "Jackson mad"; whereupon Calhoun, with an eye to the future, sought an alliance with his competitor. The upshot was that a convention held at Harrisburg in March, 1824, nominated Jackson almost unanimously and named Calhoun for the vice presidency. Hostility to the caucus became also a great asset. Tariff, internal improvements, and foreign policy were discussed in the campaign, but the real issue was the manner of selecting the President. Should he continue to be chosen by a combination of Congressmen, or should the people take matters into their own hands? Impatience with the caucus system showed itself in numerous nominations of Clay, Adams, and Jackson by sundry state conventions, legislatures, and other more or less official bodies. The supporters of Jackson, in particular, made "down with the caucus" their rallying cry and found it tremendously

THE DEATH OF "KING CAUCUS" 85

effective. In the earlier stages of the campaign the politicians, aside from Lewis and his coworkers, were unwilling to believe that Jackson could be elected. Later, however, they were forced to acknowledge his strength, and at the end the fight was really between Jackson and the field, rather than between Crawford and the field as had been anticipated.

At the beginning of November, Jackson, accompanied by his wife and traveling in a handsome coach drawn by four of the finest Hermitage thoroughbreds, set out for Washington. Hostile scribblers lost no time in contrasting this display of grandeur with the republican simplicity of Jefferson, who rode from Monticello to the capital on the back of a plantation nag without pedigree. But Jackson was not perturbed. At various points on the road he received returns from the elections, and when after four or five weeks the equipage drew up in the capital Jackson knew the general result. Calhoun had been elected vice president with little opposition. But no one of the presidential candidates had obtained an electoral majority, and the task of choosing among the highest three would, under the terms of the Constitution, devolve upon the House of Representatives. When,

86   THE REIGN OF ANDREW JACKSON

by the middle of December, the returns were all in, it was found that Jackson would have 99 votes in the electoral college, Adams 84, Crawford 41, and Clay 37.

The country awaited the 9th of February — the day of the official count — with great interest. Clay was, of course, eliminated. Crawford likewise, by reason of his poor showing and the precarious state of his health, could not expect to do more than hold his own. The contest had narrowed to Jackson and Adams, with Clay holding the balance. There were twenty-four States in the Union; the successful candidate must command the votes of thirteen.

The choice that Clay now had to make was distasteful, although not really difficult. Jackson had obtained a substantial plurality of the electoral votes; he probably had a plurality of the popular vote, although in the six States in which the electors were chosen by the Legislature the popular vote could not be computed; the Legislature of Clay's own State called upon the Congressmen from the State to give the Tennesseean its support. But Clay had felt very bitterly about the candidacy of "this military chieftain." Furthermore, he knew that if Jackson were to be elected, the country would not be disposed to take his successor from the West. Besides, Calhoun had put himself in line for the Jacksonian succession. On the other hand, Clay was not without grievances against Adams. The New Englander had captured the coveted Secretaryship of State in Monroe's Cabinet; he had taken no pains to conceal his dislike of the Kentucky "gamester in politics"; his foreign policy had been the target of many of Clay's keenest oratorical thrusts. But the country would be safe in his hands; and a popular westerner might well hope to become his successor. The decision in favor of Adams was reached with little delay and was confided to intimates almost two months before the House balloted. Though Clay's choice did not insure the election of Adams, it made that outcome extremely probable.

As the weeks passed, the situation became more tense. All the principals in the drama were at the capital — Adams as Secretary of State, Crawford as Secretary of the Treasury, Clay as Speaker of the House, Jackson as Senator — and the city was filled with followers who busied themselves in proposing combinations and making promises which, for the greater part, could not be traced to the candidates themselves. O'Neil's Tavern — graced

88   THE REIGN OF ANDREW JACKSON

by the vivacious "Peggy," who, as Mrs. John H. Eaton, was later to upset the equilibrium of the Jackson Administration — and other favorite lodging houses were the scenes of midnight conferences, intimate conversations, and mysterious comings and goings which kept their oldest and most sophisticated frequenters on the alert. "*Incedo super ignes* — I walk over fires," confided the strait-laced Adams to his diary, and not without reason. A group of Clay's friends came to the New Englander's room to urge in somewhat veiled language that their chief be promised, in return for his support, a place in the Cabinet. A Missouri representative who held the balance of power in his delegation plainly offered to swing the State for Adams if the latter would agree to retain a brother on the federal bench and be "reasonable" in the matter of patronage.

By the last week of January it was rather generally understood that Clay's strength would be thrown to Adams. Up to this time the Jackson men had refused to believe that such a thing could happen. But evidence had been piled mountain-high; adherents of both allies were openly boasting of the arrangements that had been made. The Jacksonians were furious, and the air was filled

THE DEATH OF "KING CAUCUS" 89

with recriminations. On January 28, 1825, an anonymous letter in the *Columbian Observer* of Philadelphia made the direct charge that the agents of Clay had offered the Kentuckian's support to both Jackson and Adams in return for an appointment as Secretary of State, and that, while the friends of Jackson would not descend to "such mean barter and sale," a bargain with the Adams forces had been duly closed. Clay's rage was ungovernable. Through the columns of the *National Intelligencer* he pronounced his unknown antagonist "a base and infamous calumniator, a dastard and a liar," called upon him to "unveil himself," and declared that he would hold him responsible "to all the laws which govern and regulate men of honor."

Two days later an obscure Pennsylvania Congressman by the name of George Kremer tendered his respects to "the Honorable H. Clay," avowed his authorship of the communication in question, offered to prove the truth of his charges, and closed sententiously by affirming that as a representative of the people he would "not fear to 'cry aloud and spare not' when their rights and privileges are at stake." The matter was serious, but official Washington could hardly repress a smile. Kremer was

90 THE REIGN OF ANDREW JACKSON

a thoroughly honest but grossly illiterate rustic busybody who thus far had attracted the capital's attention mainly by reason of his curiously cut leopard-skin overcoat. The real author of the charge seems to have been James Buchanan, and Kremer was simple-minded and credulous enough to be made the catspaw in the business. Clay was taken aback. Kremer significantly made no reference to the "code of honor"; and since a duel with such a personage would be an absurdity, Clay substituted a request that the House make an immediate investigation of the charges. A committee of seven was appointed. But when it summoned Kremer to give his testimony, he refused to appear, on the ground — which in the present instance was a mere pretext — that the House had no jurisdiction over the conduct of its members outside the chamber.

The truth of the matter is that Kremer was only a tool in the hands of the Jackson managers. He admitted privately to members of the committee that he did not write the letter in the *Observer*, and it was plain enough that he did not understand its purport. His promise to substantiate its contents was made in a moment of surprise, because somebody had neglected to coach him on the point.

THE DEATH OF "KING CAUCUS" 91

Finding that it could make no headway, the committee reported the fact, on the 9th of February, and the investigation was dropped. This was precisely what the Jackson managers wanted. Whatever happened, Jackson would be the gainer. "If Clay transferred his following to Adams, the charge would gain credence with the masses; if he were not made Secretary of State, it would be alleged that honest George Kremer (an ardent Jacksonian) had exposed the bargain and prevented its consummation."[1]

Was this charge of a "corrupt bargain" well founded? For a generation every public man had views on that subject for which he was ready to fight; mid-century and later historians came to conclusions of the most contradictory nature. The pros and cons are too complicated to be presented here, but certain things are fairly clear. In two elaborate speeches Clay marshaled evidence that before leaving Kentucky he decided to support Adams in preference to Jackson and Crawford. This evidence did not convince the Jacksonians; but it could hardly have been expected to do so, and nowadays it looks to be unimpeachable. It is certain that the friends of Clay approached the

[1] Turner, *Rise of the New West*, p. 268.

92 THE REIGN OF ANDREW JACKSON

Adams managers with a view to a working agreement involving the Secretaryship of State; but it is equally clear that the Jackson and Crawford men solicited Clay's support "by even more unblushing offers of political reward than those alleged against Adams." Finally it is known that Adams gave some explicit preëlection pledges, and that by doing so he drew some votes; but on the subject of an alliance with Clay he is not known to have gone further than to say to a delegation of Clay supporters that if elected by western votes he would naturally look to the West for much of the support which his Administration would need.

At noon, on the 9th of February, the Senate and House met in joint session to witness the count of the electoral vote. Spectators packed the galleries and overflowed into every available space. The first acts were of a purely formal nature. Then the envelopes were opened; the votes were counted; Calhoun was declared elected to the vice presidency; and it was announced that no candidate for the presidency had received a majority. Then the senators withdrew, and the representatives addressed themselves to the task which the Constitution devolved upon them. The members of each delegation took their seats together; the vote

THE DEATH OF "KING CAUCUS" 93

of each State was placed in a separate box on a table; and Daniel Webster and John Randolph, acting as tellers, opened the boxes and tabulated the results. No one expected the first ballot to be decisive; indeed the friends of Crawford, who were present in large numbers, were pinning their hopes to the possibility that after repeated ballotings the House would break the deadlock between Jackson and Adams by turning to their candidate. A hush fell upon the expectant assemblage as Webster rose to announce the result; and seasoned politicians could hardly trust their ears when they heard: Adams, thirteen votes; Jackson, seven; Crawford, four. An eleventh-hour change of mind by a New York representative had thrown the vote of that State into the Adams column and had thereby assured the triumph of the New Englander.

That evening Jackson and Adams came face to face at a presidential levee, Jackson with a lady on his right arm. Each man hesitated an instant, and spectators wondered what was going to happen. But those who were looking for a sensation were disappointed. Reaching out his long arm, the General said in his most cordial manner: "How do you do, Mr. Adams? I give you my left hand, for the right, as you see, is devoted to the fair: I hope you are very well, sir." The reply came in clear but icy tones: "Very well, sir; I hope General Jackson is well." It is the testimony of an unprejudiced observer that of the two, the defeated Tennesseean bore himself more graciously than the victorious New Englander.

Two days later Adams, following a conference with Monroe, invited upon his head the fires of heaven by announcing that he had decided to appoint Clay Secretary of State, "considering it due to his talents and services to the western section of the United States, whence he comes, and to the confidence in me manifested by their delegations."

CHAPTER V

THE DEMOCRATIC TRIUMPH

MONROE's Administration drew to a close in a mellow sunset of popular approval. But no prophetic genius was required to foresee that clouds of discontent and controversy would hang heavy about the head of his successor. Adams certainly did not expect it to be otherwise. "Prospects are flattering for the immediate issue," he recorded in his diary shortly before the election, "but the fearful condition of them is that success would open to a far severer trial than defeat." The darkest forebodings were more than realized. No one of our chief executives, except possibly Andrew Johnson, was ever the target of more relentless and vindictive attacks.

Adams was, in the first place, a minority President. Jackson's popular vote was probably larger; his electoral vote was certainly so; and the vote in the House of Representatives was at the last moment swung to Adams only by certain unexpected and more or less accidental developments. By thus receiving his office at the hands of a branch of Congress, in competition with a candidate who had a wider popular support, the New Englander fell heir to all the indignation that had been aroused against congressional intrigue, and especially against the selection of a President by Congressmen.

There was, in addition, the charge of a "corrupt bargain." It mattered not greatly whether the accusation was true or not. The people widely accepted it as true, and the Administration had to bear the stigma. "The coalition of Blifil and Black George, of the Puritan and the black-leg," John Randolph called the new alliance; and while Clay sought to vindicate his honor in a duel with the author of the phrase, nothing that he or Adams could do or say was able to overcome the effect upon the public mind created by the cold fact that when the Clay men turned their support to Adams their leader was forthwith made Secretary of State.

A further source of difficulty in the situation was the temperament of Adams himself. There was no abler, more honest, or more patriotic man

THE DEMOCRATIC TRIUMPH 97

in public life; yet in the presidency he was, especially at this juncture of affairs, a misfit. He was cold and reserved when every consideration called for cordiality; he was petulant when tolerance and good humor were the qualities most needful. He could neither arouse enthusiasm nor win friends. He was large visioned and adept at mapping out broad policies, but he lacked the elements of leadership requisite to carry his plans into effect. He scorned the everyday arts of politics, and by the very loftiness of his ideals he alienated support. In short, as one writer has remarked, he was "a weigher of scruples and values in a time of transition, a representative of old-school politics on the threshold of triumphant democracy. The people did not understand him, but they felt instinctively that he was not one of themselves; and, therefore, they cast him out." Nobody had ever called him "Old Hickory" or any other name indicative of popular endearment.

Clay's appointment as Secretary of State was thoroughly typical of the independent, unyielding attitude of the new Administration. Adams had not the slightest sympathy with the idea of rotation in public position: such a policy, he said, would make government "a perpetual and unremitting scramble for office." He announced that there would be no removals except such as complaint showed to be for the good of the service, and only twelve removals took place during his entire term. The spoilsmen argued and fumed. The editor of an administration newspaper warmly told the President that in consequence of his policy he would himself be removed as soon as the term for which he had been elected had expired. But entreaties and threats were alike of no avail. Even Clay could not get the removal of a naval officer guilty of unbecoming conduct. In his zeal for nonpartizanship Adams fairly leaned backwards, with the result that incompetents were shielded and the offices were left in the hands of men who, in a very large number of cases, were openly hostile to the President and to his policies.

"Less possessed of your confidence in advance than any of my predecessors," wrote Adams in his first message to Congress, "I am deeply conscious of the prospect that I shall stand more and oftener in need of your indulgence." In the principles and measures which he urged upon the legislative branch, none the less, he showed small regard for moderation or expediency. He defined the object of government to be the improvement of the

THE DEMOCRATIC TRIUMPH 99

condition of the people, and he refused to recognize in the federal Constitution restrictions which would prevent the national authorities from fulfilling this function in the highest degree. He urged not only the building of roads and canals but the establishment of a national university, the support of observatories, "the light-houses of the skies," and the exploration of the interior and of the far northwestern parts of the country. He advocated heavy protective duties on goods imported from abroad, and asked Congress to pass laws not alone for the betterment of agriculture, manufactures, and trade but for the "encouragement of the mechanic and of the elegant arts, the advancement of literature, and the progress of the sciences, ornamental and profound." He thought that the public lands should be sold at the highest prices they would bring and that the money should be used by the Government to promote the general welfare. He had no doubt of either the power or the duty of the Government to maintain a national bank.

Since the War of 1812 the Republicans, with whom Adams had been numbered, had inclined strongly toward a liberal construction of the Constitution, but none had gone to the limits marked out in this program. Besides, a strong reaction was now setting in. The President's recommendations were received in some quarters with astonishment, in some rather with amusement. Nowhere were they regarded, in their entirety, with favor. Even Clay — spokesman of nationalism though he was — could not follow his chief in his untrammeled flights. Men still widely believed that the National Government ought to spend money freely on highways, canals, and other improvements. But by his bold avowals Adams characteristically threw away support for both himself and his cause; and the era of federal initiative and management was thus hastened toward its close.

No one who knew Jackson and his political managers expected them to accept the anomalous electoral results of 1825 as expressing the real will of the nation, and it was a foregone conclusion not only that the General would again be a candidate, but that the campaign of 1828 would at once begin. The defeated Senator remained in Washington long enough to present himself at the White House on Inauguration Day and felicitate his successful rival. Then he set out on the long journey homeward. Every town through Pennsylvania and along the Ohio turned out *en masse* to greet him,

THE DEMOCRATIC TRIUMPH 101

and at Nashville he was given a prodigious reception. To friends and traveling companions he talked constantly about the election, leaving no doubt of his conviction that he had been defeated by intrigue. To a sympathetic group of passengers traveling down the Ohio with him on board the *General Neville* he declared emphatically that, if he had been willing to make the same promises and offers to Clay that Adams had made, he would that minute be in the presidential chair. If he should yet attain that dignity, he added significantly, he would do it "with clean hands." It is reported that as he spoke there was in his eye the fire of determination, such as his soldiers had seen there as he strode up and down the breastworks at New Orleans.

To this point Jackson had sought the presidency rather at the instigation of his friends than because of personal desire for the office. Now all was changed. The people had expressed their preference for him, and their will had been thwarted. Henceforth he was moved by an inflexible purpose to vindicate both his own right to the position and the right of his fellow citizens to choose their chief executive without hindrance. In this determination he was warmly backed up by his neighbors

102 THE REIGN OF ANDREW JACKSON

and advisers, and the machinery for a long, systematic, and resistless campaign was speedily put into running order. One group of managers took charge in Washington. Another set to work in New York. A third undertook to keep Pennsylvania in line. A fourth began to consolidate support in the South. At the capital the *United States Telegraph*, edited by Duff Green of Missouri, was established as a Jackson organ, and throughout the country friendly journals were set the task of keeping up an incessant fire upon the Administration and of holding the Jackson men together. Local committees were organized; pamphlets and handbills were put into circulation; receptions and public dinners were exploited, whenever possible, in the interest of the cause. First, last, and always, Jackson's candidacy was put forward as the hope and opportunity of the plain people as against the politicians.

In October the Tennessee Legislature again placed its favorite formally in nomination, and a few days later the candidate resigned his seat in the Senate in order to be more advantageously situated for carrying on his campaign. For more than a year he remained quietly at the Hermitage, dividing his attention between his blooded horses

THE DEMOCRATIC TRIUMPH 103

and dogs and his political interests. Lewis stayed at his side, partly to restrain him from outbreaks of temper or other acts that might injure his interests, partly to serve as an intermediary between him and the Washington manipulators.

Before Adams had been in the White House six months the country was divided substantially into Jackson men and anti-Jackson or administration men. The elements from which Jackson drew support were many and discordant. The backbone of his strength was the self-assertive, ambitious western Democracy, which recognized in him its truest and most eminent representative. The alliance with the Calhoun forces was kept up, although it was already jeopardized by the feeling of the South Carolinian's friends that they, and not Jackson's friends, should lead in the coming campaign. After a good deal of hesitation the supporters of Crawford came over also. Van Buren coquetted with the Adams forces for a year, and the old-line Republicans, strong in the Jeffersonian faith, brought themselves to the support of the Tennesseean with difficulty; but eventually both northern and southern wings of the Crawford contingent alined themselves against the Administration. The decision of Van Buren brought

104 THE REIGN OF ANDREW JACKSON

into the Jackson ranks a past master in party management, "the cleverest politician in a State in which the sort of politics that is concerned with the securing of elections rather than fighting for principles had grown into a science and an art." By 1826 the Jackson forces were welded into a substantial party, although for a long time their principles involved little more than hostility to Adams and enthusiasm for Jackson, and they bore no other designation than Jackson men.

The elements that were left to support the Administration were the followers of Adams and Clay. These eventually drew together under the name of National Republicans. Their strength, however, was limited, for Adams could make no appeal to the masses, even in New England; while Clay, by contributing to Jackson's defeat, had forfeited much of the popularity that would otherwise have been his.

If the story of Adams's Administration could be told in detail, it would be one long record of rancorous warfare between the President and the Jacksonian opposition in Congress. Adams, on the one hand, held inflexibly to his course, advocating policies and recommending measures which he knew had not the remotest chance of adoption;

THE DEMOCRATIC TRIUMPH 105

and, on the other hand, the opposition—which in the last two years of the Administration controlled the Senate as well as the House of Representatives — balked at no act that would humiliate the President and make capital for its western idol. At the outset the Jacksonians tried to hold up the confirmation of Clay. It fell furiously, and quite without discrimination, upon the President's great scheme of national improvements, professing to see in it evidence of an insatiable desire for "concentration." In the discussion of a proposed amendment to the Constitution providing for direct election of the President by the people it was constantly assumed and frequently stated that Adams had no moral right to the position which he occupied. The President's decision to send delegates to the Panama Congress of 1826 raised a storm of acrimonious debate and brought the Administration's enemies into closer unison. To cap the climax, Adams was solemnly charged with abuse of the federal patronage, and in the Senate six bills for the remedy of the President's pernicious practices were brought in by Benton in a single batch! Adams was able and honest, but he got no credit from his opponents for these qualities. He, in turn, displayed little magnanimity; and in refusing

106 THE REIGN OF ANDREW JACKSON

to shape his policies and methods to meet the conditions under which he had to work, he fell short of the highest statesmanship.

As election year approached, it became clear that the people would at last have an opportunity to make a direct choice between Adams and Jackson. Each candidate was formally nominated by sundry legislatures and other bodies; no one so much as suggested nomination by congressional caucus. In the early months of 1828 the campaign rapidly rose to an extraordinary level of vigor and public interest. Each party group became bitter and personal in its attacks upon the other; in our entire political history there have been not more than two or three campaigns so smirched with vituperation and abuse. The Jackson papers and stump speakers laid great stress on Adams's aristocratic temperament, denounced his policies as President, and exploited the "corrupt bargain" charge with all possible ingenuity.

On the other hand, the Adams-Clay forces dragged forth in long array Jackson's quarrels, duels, and rough-and-tumble encounters to prove that he was not fit to be President; they distributed handbills decorated with coffins bearing the names of the candidate's victims; they cited scores

THE DEMOCRATIC TRIUMPH 107

of actions, from the execution of mutinous militiamen in the Creek War to the quarrel with Callava, to show his arbitrary disposition; and they strove in a most malicious manner to undermine his popularity by breaking down his personal reputation, and even that of his wife and of his mother. It has been said that "the reader of old newspaper files and pamphlet collections of the Adamsite persuasion, in the absence of other knowledge, would gather that Jackson was a usurper, an adulterer, a gambler, a cock-fighter, a brawler, a drunkard, and withal a murderer of the most cruel and blood-thirsty description." Issues — tariff, internal improvements, foreign policy, slavery — receded into the background; the campaign became for all practical purposes a personal contest between the Tennessee soldier and the two statesmen whom he accused of bargain and corruption. "Hurrah for Jackson!" was the beginning and end of the creed of the masses bent on the Tennesseean's election.

Jackson never wearied of saying that he was "no politician." He was, none the less, one of the most forceful and successful politicians that the country has known. He was fortunate in being able to personify a cause which was grounded deeply in the feelings and opinions of the people,

108 THE REIGN OF ANDREW JACKSON

and also in being able to command the services of a large group of tireless and skillful national and local managers. He was willing to leave to these managers the infinite details of his campaign. But he kept in close touch with them and their subordinates, and upon occasion he did not hesitate to take personal command. In politics, as in war, he was imperious; persons not willing to support him with all their might, and without question or quibble, he preferred to see on the other side. Throughout the campaign his opponents hoped, and his friends feared, that he would commit some deed of anger that would ruin his chances of election. The temptation was strong, especially when the circumstances of his marriage were dragged into the controversy. But while he chafed inwardly, and sometimes expressed himself with more force than elegance in the presence of his friends, he maintained an outward calm and dignity. His bitterest feeling was reserved for Clay, who was known to be the chief inspirer of the National Republicans' mud-slinging campaign. But he felt that Adams had it in his power to put a stop to the slanders that were set in circulation, had he cared to do so.

As the campaign drew to a close, circumstances

THE DEMOCRATIC TRIUMPH 109

pointed with increasing sureness to the triumph of the Jackson forces. Adams, foreseeing the end, found solace in harsh and sometimes picturesque entries in his diary. A group of opposition Congressmen he pronounced "skunks of party slander." Calhoun he described as "stimulated to frenzy by success, flattery, and premature advancement; governed by no steady principle, but sagacious to seize upon every prevailing popular breeze to swell his own sails." Clay, likewise, became petulant and gloomy. In the last two months of the canvass Jackson ordered a general onslaught upon Kentucky, and when finally it was affirmed that the State had been "carried out from under" its accustomed master, Clay knew only too well that the boast was true. To Adams's assurances that after four years of Jackson the country would gladly turn to the Kentuckian, the latter could only reply that there would, indeed, be a reaction, but that before another President would be taken from the West he would be too old; and it was with difficulty that Adams persuaded him not to retire immediately from the Cabinet.

The results of the contest fully bore out the apprehensions of the Administration. Jackson received nearly 140,000 more popular votes than

110 THE REIGN OF ANDREW JACKSON

Adams and carried every State south of the Potomac and west of the Alleghanies. He carried Pennsylvania also by a vote of two to one and divided about equally with his opponent the votes of New York and Maryland. Only New England held fast for Adams. As one writer has facetiously remarked, "It took a New England conscience to hold a follower in line for the New England candidate." The total electoral vote was 178 for Jackson and 83 for Adams. Calhoun was easily reëlected to the vice presidency. Both branches of Congress remained under the control of Jackson's partizans.

Months before the election, congratulatory messages began to pour into the Hermitage. Some came from old friends and disinterested well-wishers, many from prospective seekers of office or of other favors. Influential people in the East, and especially at the capital, hastened to express their desire to be of service to the Jacksons in the new life to which they were about to be called. In the list one notes with interest the names of General Thomas Cadwalader of Philadelphia, salaried lobbyist for the United States Bank, and Senator Robert Y. Hayne, the future South Carolina nullifier.

THE DEMOCRATIC TRIUMPH 111

Returns sufficiently complete to leave no doubt of Jackson's election reached the Hermitage on the 9th of December. That afternoon, Lewis, Carroll, and a few other members of the "general headquarters staff" gathered at the Jackson home to review the situation and look over the bulky correspondence that had come in. "General Jackson," reports Lewis, "showed no elation. In fact, he had for some time considered his election certain, the only question in his mind being the extent of the majority. When he finished looking over the summary by States, his only remark was that Isaac Hill, considering the odds against him, had done wonders in New Hampshire!"

When, two weeks later, the final returns were received, leading Tennesseeans decided to give a reception, banquet, and ball which would outshine any social occasion in the annals of the Southwest. Just as arrangements were completed, however, Mrs. Jackson, who had long been in failing health, suffered an attack of heart trouble; and at the very hour when the General was to have been received, amid all the trappings of civil and military splendor, with the huzzas of his neighbors, friends, and admirers, he was sitting tearless, speechless, and almost expressionless by the corpse of his life companion. Long after the beloved one had been laid to rest in the Hermitage garden amid the rosebushes she had planted, the President-elect continued as one benumbed. He never gave up the idea that his wife had been killed by worry over the attacks made upon him and upon her by the Adams newspapers — that, as he expressed it, she was "murdered by slanders that pierced her heart." Only under continued prodding from Lewis and other friends did he recall himself to his great task and set about preparing for the arduous winter journey to Washington, composing his inaugural address, selecting his Cabinet, and laying plans for the reorganization of the federal Civil Service on lines already definitely in his mind.

CHAPTER VI

THE "REIGN" BEGINS

JACKSON'S election to the presidency in 1828 was correctly described by Senator Benton as "a triumph of democratic principle, and an assertion of the people's right to govern themselves." Jefferson in his day was a candidate of the masses, and his triumph over John Adams in 1800 was received with great public acclaim. Yet the Virginian was at best an aristocratic sort of democrat; he was never in the fullest sense a man of the people. Neither Madison nor Monroe inspired enthusiasm, and for John Quincy Adams even New Englanders voted, as Ezekiel Webster confessed, from a cold sense of duty. Jackson was, as no President before him, the choice of the masses. His popular vote in 1824 revealed not only his personal popularity but the growing power of the democratic elements in the nation, and his defeat in the House of Representatives only strengthened

114 THE REIGN OF ANDREW JACKSON

his own and the people's determination to be finally victorious. The untrained, self-willed, passionate frontier soldier came to power in 1828 as the standard bearer of a mighty democratic uprising which was destined before it ran its course to break down oligarchical party organizations, to liberalize state and local governments, and to turn the stream of national politics into wholly new channels. It was futile for men of the old school to protest and to prophesy misfortune for the country under its new rulers. The people had spoken, and this time the people's will was not to be denied.

Still haggard from his recent personal loss, the President-elect set out for Washington, at the middle of January, 1829. With him went his nephew, Andrew Jackson Donelson, who was to be his private secretary; Mrs. Donelson, who was to preside over the executive mansion; an accomplished niece of Mrs. Jackson, who was to be of social assistance; an artist by the name of Earl, who resided at the White House throughout Jackson's two Administrations, engaged continually in painting portraits of the General; and, finally, the faithful Major Lewis, whose intention was merely to attend the inauguration and then return to his plantation. The puffing little steamboat

THE "REIGN" BEGINS 115

on which the party traveled down the Cumberland and up the Ohio was saluted and cheered a hundred times a day; at Louisville, Cincinnati, and Pittsburgh there were great outpourings of demonstrative citizens. Duff Green, one of the party managers, proposed that a great cavalcade should meet the victor at Pittsburgh and escort him by relays to the capital. On Van Buren's advice the plan was abandoned. But as the party passed along the National Road toward its destination it was accorded an ovation which left nothing to be desired as an evidence of the public favor.

Arrived in Washington, on the 11th of February — the day on which the electoral votes were counted in the Senate — Jackson and his friends found temporary lodgings at the Indian Queen Tavern, commonly known as "the Wigwam." During the next three weeks the old inn was the scene of unwonted activity. Office seekers besieged it morning, noon, and night; politicians came to ask favors or give advice; exponents of every sort of cause watched for opportunities to obtain promises of presidential support; scores of the curious came with no other purpose than to see what a backwoods President looked like. "The city is full of speculation and speculators," wrote

116 THE REIGN OF ANDREW JACKSON

Daniel Webster to his sister-in-law a few days after Jackson's arrival; "a great multitude, too many to be fed without a miracle, are already in the city, hungry for office. Especially, I learn that the typographical corps is assembled in great force. From New Hampshire, our friend Hill; from Boston, Mr. Greene . . . and from everywhere else somebody else. So many friends ready to advise, and whose advice is so disinterested, make somewhat of a numerous council about the President-elect; and, if report be true, it is a council which only makes that darker which was dark enough before."

To all, Jackson was accessible. But he was not communicative, and up to Inauguration Day people were left to speculate not only upon the truth of the rumor that there was to be a "full sweep" in the offices but upon the new Administration's attitude on public questions in general. Even Isaac Hill, a warm friend and supporter, was obliged to write to an acquaintance four days before the inauguration that Jackson had little to say about the future, "except in a general way." The men with whom the Executive-elect was daily closeted were Major Lewis and Senators Eaton and White. Van Buren would have been of the

THE "REIGN" BEGINS 117

number, had not his recently assumed duties as Governor kept him at Albany. He was ably represented, however, by James A. Hamilton, a son of Alexander Hamilton, to whose correspondence we owe most of what we know about the laying of the plans for the new Administration.

The most pressing question was the personnel of the Cabinet. Upon only one appointment was Jackson fully determined when he reached Washington: Van Buren was to be Secretary of State. The "little magician" had been influential in turning New York from Crawford to Jackson; he had resigned his seat in the Senate and run for the governorship with a view to uniting the party for Jackson's benefit; he was the cleverest politician and, next to Calhoun, the ablest man, in the Democratic ranks. When offered the chief place in the Cabinet he promptly accepted. Edward Livingston was given his choice of the remaining positions, but preferred to accept an election to the Senate. With due regard for personal susceptibilities and sectional interests, the list was then completed. A Pennsylvania Congressman, Samuel D. Ingham, became Secretary of the Treasury; Senator John H. Eaton was made Secretary of War; a Calhoun supporter from North

118 THE REIGN OF ANDREW JACKSON

Carolina, John Branch, was given the Navy portfolio; Senator John M. Berrien of Georgia became Attorney-General; and William T. Barry of Kentucky was appointed Postmaster-General, after the incumbent, John McLean, refused to accept the policy of a clean slate in the department. The appointments were kept secret until one week before the inauguration, when they were announced in the party organ at the capital, Duff Green's *United States Telegraph.*

Everywhere the list caused consternation. Van Buren's was the only name of distinction in it; and only one of the appointees had had experience in the administration of national affairs. Hamilton pronounced the group "the most unintellectual Cabinet we ever had." Van Buren doubted whether he ought to have accepted a seat in such company. A crowning expression of dissatisfaction came from the Tennessee delegation in Congress, which formally protested against the appointment of Eaton. But the President-elect was not to be swayed. His ideas of administrative efficiency were not highly developed, and he believed that his Cabinet would prove equal to all demands made upon it. Not the least of its virtues in his eyes was the fact that, although nearly evenly

THE "REIGN" BEGINS 119

divided between his own followers and the friends of Calhoun, it contained not one person who was not an uncompromising anti-Clay man.

Meanwhile a motley army of office seekers, personal friends, and sightseers — to the number of ten or fifteen thousand — poured into Washington to see the old régime of Virginia, New York, and Massachusetts go out and the new régime of the people come in. "A monstrous crowd of people," wrote Webster on Inauguration Day, "is in the city. I never saw anything like it before. Persons have come five hundred miles to see General Jackson, and they really seem to think that the country is rescued from some dreadful danger." Another observer, who was also not a Jacksonian, wrote[1]:

No one who was in Washington at the time of General Jackson's inauguration is likely to forget that period to the day of his death. To us, who had witnessed the quiet and orderly period of the Adams Administration, it seemed as if half the nation had rushed at once into the capital. It was like the inundation of the northern barbarians into Rome, save that the tumultuous tide came in from a different point of the compass. The West and the South seemed to have precipitated themselves upon the North and overwhelmed it. . . .

[1] Parton, *Life of Andrew Jackson*, vol. III, p. 168.

120 THE REIGN OF ANDREW JACKSON

Strange faces filled every public place, and every face seemed to bear defiance on its brow. It appeared to me that every Jackson editor in the country was on the spot. They swarmed, especially in the lobbies of the House, an expectant host, a sort of Prætorian band, which, having borne in upon their shields their idolized leader, claimed the reward of the hard-fought contest.

The 4th of March dawned clear and balmy. "By ten o'clock," says an eye-witness, "the Avenue was crowded with carriages of every description, from the splendid baronet and coach, down to wagons and carts, filled with women and children, some in finery and some in rags, for it was the People's president." The great square which now separates the Capitol and the Library of Congress was in Jackson's day shut in by a picket fence. This enclosure was filled with people — "a vast agitated sea" — while in all directions the slopes of Capitol Hill were thickly occupied. At noon watchers on the west portico, looking down Pennsylvania Avenue, saw a group of gentlemen issue from the Indian Queen and thread its way slowly up the hill. All wore their hats except one tall, dignified, white-haired figure in the middle, who was quickly recognized as Jackson. Passing through the building, the party, reinforced by Chief Justice Marshall and certain

THE "REIGN" BEGINS

other dignitaries, emerged upon the east portico, amid the deafening cheers of the spectators. The President-elect bowed gravely, and, stepping forward to a small cloth-covered table, read in a low voice the inaugural address; the aged Chief Justice, "whose life was a protest against the political views of the Jackson party," administered the oath of office; and the ceremony was brought to a close in the customary manner by the new Executive kissing the Bible. Francis Scott Key, watching the scene from one of the gates, was moved to exclaim: "It is beautiful, it is sublime."

Thus far the people had been sufficiently impressed by the dignity of the occasion to keep their places and preserve a reasonable silence. But when the executive party started to withdraw, men, women, and children rushed past the police and scrambled up the steps in a wild effort to reach their adored leader and grasp his hand. Disheveled and panting, the President finally reached a gate at which his horse was in waiting; and, mounting with difficulty, he set off for the White House, followed by a promiscuous multitude, "countrymen, farmers, gentlemen, mounted and unmounted, boys, women, and children, black and white."

122 THE REIGN OF ANDREW JACKSON

The late President had no part in the day's proceedings. On arriving in Washington, Jackson had refused to make the usual call of the incoming upon the outgoing Executive, mainly because he held Adams responsible for the newspaper virulence which had caused Mrs. Jackson such distress and had possibly shortened her life. Deserted by all save his most intimate friends, the New Englander faced the last hours of his Administration in bitterness. His diary bears ample evidence of his ill-humor and chagrin. On the 3d of March he took up his residence on Meridian Hill, near the western limits of the city; and thence he did not venture until the festivities of the ensuing day were ended. No amount of effort on the part of mediators ever availed to bring about a reconciliation between him and his successor.

According to custom, the inaugural program came to an end with a reception at the White House; and arrangements were made to entertain a large number of guests. Police control, however, proved wholly inadequate, and when the throng that followed the President up the Avenue reached the executive grounds it engulfed the mansion and poured in by windows as well as doors,

THE "REIGN" BEGINS

until the reception rooms were packed to suffocation. Other guests, bidden and unbidden — "statesmen and stable-boys, fine ladies and washerwomen, white people and blacks" — continued for hours to besiege the doors. "I never saw such a mixture," records Judge Story; "the reign of King Mob seemed triumphant. I was glad to escape from the scene as soon as possible." The President, too, after being jostled for an hour, very willingly made his way by a side entrance to the street and thence to his hotel.

A profusion of refreshments, including barrels of orange punch, had been provided; and an attempt to serve the guests led to a veritable saturnalia. Waiters emerging from doors with loaded trays were borne to the floor by the crush; china and glassware were smashed; gallons of punch were spilled on the carpets; in their eagerness to be served men in muddy boots leaped upon damask-covered chairs, overturned tables, and brushed bric-à-brac from mantles and walls. "It would have done Mr. Wilberforce's heart good," writes a cynical observer, "to have seen a stout black wench eating in this free country a jelly with a gold spoon at the President's House." Only when some thoughtful person directed that tubs of punch be placed here and there on the lawn was the congestion indoors relieved. When it was all over, the White House resembled a pigsty. "Several thousand dollars' worth of broken china and cut glass and many bleeding noses attested the fierceness of the struggle." It was the people's day, and it was of no avail for fastidious Adamsites to lift their eyebrows in ridicule or scorn.

Those in whom the establishment of the new order aroused keenest apprehension were the officeholders. A favorite theme of the Jackson forces during the late campaign was the abuses of the patronage, and the General came into office fully convinced that an overhauling of the civil service would be one of the greatest contributions that he could make to his country's welfare. Even if he had been less sure of this than he was, the pressure which office seekers and their friends brought to bear upon him would have been irresistible. Four-fifths of the people who flocked to Washington at inauguration time were seekers after office for themselves or their friends, and from every county and town the country over came pleas of service rendered and claims for reward. But Jackson needed little urging. He thought, and rightly, that many of the incumbents

THE "REIGN" BEGINS 125

had grown lax in the performance of their duties, if indeed they had ever been anything else, and that fresh blood was needed in the government employ. He believed that short terms and rapid rotation made for alertness and efficiency. He felt that one man had as much right to public office as another, and he was so unacquainted with the tasks of administration as to suppose all honest citizens equally capable of serving their fellowmen in public station. As for the grievances of persons removed, his view was that "no individual wrong is done by removal, since neither appointment to nor continuance in office is a matter of right."

Shortly after the election Major Lewis wrote to a friend that the General was "resolved on making a pretty clean sweep of the departments." It is expected, he added, that "he will cleanse the Augean stables, and I feel pretty confident that he will not disappoint the popular expectation in this particular." If a complete overturn was ever really contemplated, the plan was not followed up; and it is more than possible that it was Van Buren who marked off the limits beyond which it would not be expedient to go. None the less, Jackson's removals far exceeded those made by his predecessors. Speaking broadly, the power of removal had never yet been exercised in the Federal Government with offensive partizanship. Even under Jefferson, when the holders of half of the offices were changed in the space of four years, there were few removals for political reasons.

No sooner was Jackson in office, however, than wholesale proscription began. The ax fell in every department and bureau, and cut off chiefs and clerks with equal lack of mercy. Age and experience counted rather against a man than in his favor, and rarely was any reason given for removal other than that some one else wanted the place. When Congress met, in December, it was estimated that a thousand persons had been ousted; and during the first year of the Administration the number is said to have reached two thousand. The Post-Office Department and the Customs Service were purged with special severity. The sole principle on which the new appointees were selected was loyalty to Jackson. Practically all were inexperienced, most were incompetent, and several proved dishonest.

"There has been," wrote the President in his journal a few weeks after the inauguration, "a great noise made about removals." Protest arose not only from the proscribed and their friends, but from the Adams-Clay forces generally, and even from some of the more moderate Jacksonians. "Were it not for the outdoor popularity of General Jackson," wrote Webster, "the Senate would have negatived more than half his nominations." As it was, many were rejected; and some of the worst were, under pressure, withdrawn. On the general principle the President held his ground. "It is rotation in office," he again and again asserted in all honesty, "that will perpetuate our liberty," and from this conviction no amount of argument or painful experience could shake him. After 1830 one hears less about the subject, but only because the novelty and glamor of the new régime had worn off.

Jackson was not the author of the spoils system. The device of using the offices as rewards for political service had long been familiar in the state and local governments, notably in New York. What Jackson and his friends did was simply to carry over the spoils principle into the National Government. No more unfortunate step was ever taken by an American President; the task of undoing the mischief has been long and laborious. Yet the spoils system was probably an inevitable feature of the new rule of the people; at all events,

128 THE REIGN OF ANDREW JACKSON

it was accepted by all parties and sanctioned by public sentiment for more than half a century.

Like Philip II of Spain, who worked twelve hours a day at the business of being a King, Jackson took the duties of his exalted post very seriously. No man had ever accused him of laxness in public office, civil or military; on the contrary, his superiors commonly considered themselves fortunate if they could induce or compel him to keep his energies within reasonable bounds. As President he was not without distressing shortcomings. He was self-willed, prejudiced, credulous, petulant. But he was honest, and he was industrious. No President ever kept a closer watch upon Congress to see that the rights of the executive were not invaded or the will of the people thwarted; and his vigilance was rewarded, not only by his success in vindicating the independence of the executive in a conflict whose effects are felt to this day, but by the very respectable amount of legislation which he contrived to obtain in the furtherance of what he believed to be the public welfare. When a rebellious Congress took the bit in its teeth, he never hesitated to crack the whip over its head. Sometimes the pressure was applied indirectly, but with none the less effect. One of

THE "REIGN" BEGINS 129

the first acts of the Senate to arouse strong feelings in the White House was the rejection of the nomination of Isaac Hill to be Second Comptroller of the Treasury. A New Hampshire senatorship soon falling vacant, the President deftly brought about the election of Hill to the position; and many a gala hour he had in later days as Lewis and other witnesses described the chagrin of the senators at being obliged to accept as one of their colleagues a man whom they had adjudged unfit for a less important office.

Much thought had been bestowed upon the composition of the Cabinet, and some of the President's warmest supporters urged that he should make use of the group as a council of state, after the manner of his predecessors. Jackson's purposes, however, ran in a different direction. He had been on intimate terms with fewer than half of the members, and he saw no reason why these men, some of whom were primarily the friends of Calhoun, should be allowed to supplant old confidants like Lewis. Let them, he reasoned, go about their appointed tasks as heads of the administrative departments, while he looked for counsel whithersoever he desired. Hence the official Cabinet fell into the background, and after a few weeks the practice of holding meetings was dropped.

As advisers on party affairs and on matters of general policy the President drew about himself a heterogeneous group of men which the public labeled the "Kitchen Cabinet." Included in the number were the two members of the regular Cabinet in whom Jackson had implicit confidence, Van Buren and Eaton. Isaac Hill was a member. Amos Kendall, a New Englander who had lately edited a Jackson paper in Kentucky, and who now found his reward in the fourth auditorship of the Treasury, was another. William B. Lewis, prevailed upon by Jackson to accept another auditorship along with Kendall, rather than to follow out his original intention to return to his Tennessee plantation, was not only in the Kitchen Cabinet but was also a member of the President's household. Duff Green, editor of the *Telegraph*, and A. J. Donelson, the President's nephew and secretary, were included in the group; as was also Francis P. Blair after, in 1830, he became editor of the new administration organ, the *Globe*. It was the popular impression that the influence of these men, especially of Lewis and Kendall, was very great — that, indeed, they virtually ruled the

THE "REIGN" BEGINS 131

country. There was some truth in the supposition. In matters upon which his mind was not fully made up, Jackson was easily swayed; and his most intimate "Kitchen" advisers were adepts at playing upon his likes and dislikes. He, however, always resented the insinuation that he was not his own master, and all testimony goes to show that when he was once resolved upon a given course his friends were just as powerless to stop him as were his enemies.

The Jacksonians were carried into office on a great wave of popular enthusiasm, and for the time being all the powers of government were theirs. None the less, their position was imperiled almost from the beginning by a breach within the administration ranks. Calhoun had contented himself with reëlection to the vice presidency in 1828 on the understanding that, after Jackson should have had one term, the road to the White House would be left clear for himself. Probably Jackson, when elected, fully expected Calhoun to be his successor. Before long, however, the South Carolinian was given ground for apprehension. Men began to talk about a second term for Jackson, and the White House gave no indication of disapproval. Even more disconcerting was the large place taken in the new régime by Van Buren. The "little magician" held the chief post in the Cabinet; he was in the confidence of the President as Calhoun was not; there were multiplying indications that he was aiming at the presidency; and if he were to enter the race he would be hard to beat, for by general admission he was the country's most astute politician. With every month that passed the Vice President's star was in graver danger of eclipse.

Several curious circumstances worked together to widen the breach between the Calhoun and Van Buren elements and at the same time to bring the President definitely into the ranks of the New Yorker's supporters. One was the controversy over the social status of "Peggy" Eaton. Peggy was the daughter of a tavern keeper, William O'Neil, at whose hostelry both Jackson and Eaton had lived when they were senators. Her first husband, a purser in the navy, committed suicide at sea; and Washington gossips said that he was driven to the act by chagrin caused by his wife's misconduct, both before and after her marriage. On the eve of Jackson's inauguration the widow became Mrs. Eaton, and certain disagreeable rumors connecting the names of the two were con-

THE "REIGN" BEGINS 133

firmed in the public mind. When Eaton was made Secretary of War, society shrugged its shoulders and wondered what sort of figure "Peg O'Neil" would cut in Cabinet circles. The question was soon answered. At the first official functions Mrs. Eaton was received with studied neglect by the wives of the other Cabinet officers; and all refused either to call on her or to receive her in their homes.

Jackson was furious. It was enough for him that Mrs. Jackson had thought well of the suspected woman, and all his gallantry rose in her defense. Professing to regard the attitude of the protesters as nothing less than an affront to his Administration, he called upon the men of the Cabinet, and upon the Vice President, to remonstrate with their wives in Mrs. Eaton's behalf. But if any such remonstrances were made, nothing came of them. "For once in his life, Andrew Jackson was defeated. Creeks and Spaniards and Redcoats he could conquer, but the ladies of Washington never surrendered, and Peggy Eaton though her affairs became a national question, never got into Washington society."[1] The political effect of the episode was considerable. Van Buren was

[1] Brown, *Andrew Jackson*, p. 127.

a widower, and, having no family to object, he showed Mrs. Eaton all possible courtesy. On the other hand, Mrs. Calhoun was the leader of those who refused Mrs. Eaton recognition. Jackson was not slow to note these facts, and his opinion of Van Buren steadily rose, while he set down Calhoun as an obdurate member of the "conspiracy."

Throughout the winter of 1829-30 the Calhoun and Van Buren factions kept up a contest which daily became more acrimonious and open. Already the clique around the President had secretly decided that in 1832 he must run again, with Van Buren as a mate, and that the New Yorker should be the presidential candidate in 1836. Though irritated by the Vice President's conduct in the Eaton affair and in other matters, Jackson threw over the understanding of 1828 with reluctance. Even when, on the last day of 1829, his friends, alarmed by the state of his health, persuaded him to write a letter to a Tennessee judge warmly commending Van Buren and expressing grave doubts about the South Carolinian — a statement which, in the event of worst fears being realized, would be of the utmost value to the Van Buren men — he was unwilling to go the full length of an open break.

But Lewis and his coworkers were craftily laying

THE "REIGN" BEGINS

the train of powder that would lead to an explosion, and in the spring of 1830 they were ready to apply the match. When the President had been worked up to the right stage of suspicion, it was suddenly made known to him that it was Calhoun, not Crawford, who in Monroe's Cabinet circle in 1818 had urged that the conqueror of Florida be censured for his bold deeds. This had the full effect desired. Jackson made a peremptory demand upon the Vice President for an explanation of his perfidy. Calhoun responded in a letter which explained and explained, yet got nowhere. Whereupon Jackson replied in a haughty communication, manifestly prepared by the men who were engineering the whole business, declaring the former Secretary guilty of the most reprehensible duplicity and severing all relations with him. This meant the end of Calhoun's hopes, at all events for the present. He could never be President while Jackson's influence lasted. Van Buren had won; and the embittered South Carolinian could only turn for solace to the nullification movement, in which he was already deeply engulfed.

Pursuing their plans to the final stroke, the Administration managers forced a reconstruction of the Cabinet, and all of Calhoun's supporters were displaced. Louis McLane of Delaware became Secretary of the Treasury; Lewis Cass of Michigan, Secretary of War; Levi Woodbury of New Hampshire, Secretary of the Navy; and Roger B. Taney of Maryland, Attorney-General. Van Buren also retired, in conformity with Jackson's announced intention not to have any one in the Cabinet who was a candidate for the succession; and Edward Livingston, Jackson's old Louisiana friend, became Secretary of State.

It was decided that a fitting post for a successor while awaiting his turn — particularly for one who was not popular — would be the ministership to Great Britain; and Van Buren duly traveled to London to take up the duties of this position. But when the appointment was submitted to the Senate, Calhoun's friends adroitly managed matters so that the Vice President should have the satisfaction of preventing confirmation by his casting vote. "It will kill him, sir, kill him dead," declared the vengeful South Carolinian to a doubting friend. "He will never kick, sir, never kick." But no greater tactical error could have been committed. Benton showed the keener insight when he informed the jubilant Calhoun men that they had "broken a minister," only to elect a Vice President.

CHAPTER VII

THE WEBSTER-HAYNE DEBATE

THE United States came out of her second war with Great Britain a proud and fearless nation, though her record was not, on its face, glorious. She went to war shockingly unprepared; the people were of divided opinion, and one great section was in open revolt; the military leaders were without distinction; the soldiery was poorly trained and equipped; finances were disordered; the operations on land were mostly failures; and the privateers, which achieved wonders in the early stages of the contest, were driven to cover long before the close; for the restoration of peace the nation had to thank England's war weariness far more than her own successes; and the Treaty of Ghent did not so much as mention impressment, captures, or any of the other matters mainly at issue when the war was begun. Peace, however, brought gratitude, enthusiasm, optimism. Defeats were quickly forgotten; and

138 THE REIGN OF ANDREW JACKSON

Jackson's victory at New Orleans atoned for the humiliations of years. After all, the contest had been victorious in its larger outcome, for the new world conditions were such as to insure that the claims and practices which had troubled the relations of the United States and Great Britain would never be revived. The carpings of critics were drowned in the public rejoicings. The Hartford Convention dissolved unwept and unsung. Flushed with pride and confidence, the country entered upon a new and richer epoch.

The dominant tone of this dawning period was nationalism. The nation was to be made great and rich and free; sectional interests and ambitions were to be merged in the greater national purpose. Congress voiced the sentiment of the day by freely laying tariffs to protect newly risen manufactures, by appropriating money for "internal improvements," by establishing a second United States Bank, and by giving full support to the annexation of territory for the adjustment of border difficulties and the extension of the country to its natural frontiers.

Under the leadership of John Marshall, the Supreme Court handed down an imposing series of decisions restricting the powers of the States and throwing open the floodgates for the expansion of national functions and activities. Statesmen of all sections put the nation first in their plans and policies as they had not always done in earlier days. John C. Calhoun was destined shortly to take rank as the greatest of sectionalists. Nevertheless, between 1815 and 1820 he voted for protective tariffs, brought in a great bill for internal improvements, and won from John Quincy Adams praise for being "above all sectional . . . prejudices more than any other statesman of this union" with whom he "had ever acted."

The differences between the nationalist and state rights schools were, however, deep-rooted — altogether too fundamental to be obliterated by even the nationalizing swing of the war period; and in a brief time the old controversy of Hamilton and Jefferson was renewed on the former lines. The pull of political tradition and of sectional interest was too strong to be resisted. In the commercial and industrial East tradition and interest supported, in general, the doctrine of broad national powers; and the same was true of the West and Northwest. The South, however, inclined to limited national powers, large functions for the States, and such a construction of the Constitution as would give the benefit of the doubt in all cases to the States.

The political theory current south of the Potomac and the Ohio made of state rights a fetish. Yet the powerful sectional reaction which set in after 1820 against the nationalizing tendency had as its main impetus the injustice which the Southern people felt had been done to them through the use of the nation's larger powers. They objected to the protective tariff as a device which not only brought the South no benefit but interfered with its markets and raised the cost of certain of its staple supplies. They opposed internal improvements at national expense because of their consolidating tendency, and because few of the projects carried out were of large advantage to the Southern people. They regarded the National Bank as at best useless; and they resisted federal legislation imposing restrictions on slavery as prejudicial to vested rights in the "peculiar institution."

After 1820 the pendulum swung rapidly back toward particularism. State rights sentiment was freely expressed by men, both Southern and Northern, whose views commanded respect; and in more than one State — notably in Ohio and Georgia —

THE WEBSTER-HAYNE DEBATE 141

bold actions proclaimed this sentiment to be no mere matter of academic opinion. Ohio in 1819 forcibly collected a tax on the United States Bank in defiance of the Supreme Court's decision in the case of M'Culloch *vs.* Maryland; and in 1821 her Legislature reaffirmed the doctrines of the Virginia and Kentucky resolutions and persisted in resistance, even after the Supreme Court had rendered a decision[1] specifically against the position which the State had taken. Judge Roane of Virginia, in a series of articles in the *Richmond Enquirer*, argued that the Federal Union was a compact among the States and that the nationalistic reasoning of his fellow Virginian, Marshall, in the foregoing decisions was false; and Jefferson heartily endorsed his views. In Cohens *vs.* Virginia, in 1821, the Supreme Court held that it had appellate jurisdiction in a case decided by a state court where the Constitution and laws of the United States were involved, even though a State was a party; whereupon the Virginia House of Delegates declared that the State's lawyers had been right in their contention that final construction of the Constitution lay with the courts of the States. Jefferson, also, gave this assertion his

[1] Osborn *vs.* Bank of the United States.

support, and denounced the centralizing tendencies of the Judiciary, "which, working like gravity without any intermission, is to press us at last into one consolidated mass."

In 1825 Jefferson actually proposed that the Virginia Legislature should pass a set of resolutions pronouncing null and void the whole body of federal laws on the subject of internal improvements. The Georgia Legislature, aroused by growing antislavery activities in the North, declared in 1827 that the remedy lay in "a firm and determined union of the people and the States of the South" against interference with the institutions of that section of the country. Already Georgia had placed herself in an attitude of resistance to the Federal Government upon the rights of the Indians within her borders, and within the next decade she repeatedly nullified decisions of the federal courts on this subject. In 1828 the South Carolina Legislature adopted a series of eight resolutions denouncing the lately enacted "tariff of abominations," and a report, originally drafted by Calhoun and commonly known as *The South Carolina Exposition*, in which were to be found all of the essentials of the constitutional argument underlying the nullification movement of 1832.

THE WEBSTER-HAYNE DEBATE 143

When Jackson went into the White House, the country was therefore fairly buzzing with discussions of constitutional questions. What was the true character of the Constitution and of the Union established under it? Were the States sovereign? Who should determine the limits of state and federal powers? What remedy had a State against unconstitutional measures of the National Government? Who should say when an act was unconstitutional?

The South, in particular, was in an irritable frame of mind. Agriculture was in a state of depression; manufacturing was not developing as had been expected; the steadily mounting tariffs were working economic disadvantage; the triumph of members of Congress and of the Supreme Court who favored a loose construction of the Constitution indicated that there would be no end of acts and decisions contrary to what the South regarded as her own interests. Some apprehensive people looked to Jackson for reassurance. But his first message to Congress assumed that the tariff would continue as it was, and, indeed, gave no promise of relief in any direction.

It was at this juncture that the whole controversy flared up unexpectedly in one of the greatest debates ever heard on the floor of our Congress or in the legislative halls of any country. On December 29, 1829, Senator Samuel A. Foote of Connecticut offered an innocent-looking resolution proposing a temporary restriction of the sale of public lands to such lands as had already been placed on the market. The suggestion was immediately resented by western members, who professed to see in it a desire to check the drain of eastern population to the West; and upon the reconvening of Congress following the Christmas recess Senator Benton of Missouri voiced in no uncertain terms the indignation of his State and section. The discussion might easily have led to nothing more than the laying of the resolution on the table; and in that event we should never have heard of it. But it happened that one of the senators from South Carolina, Robert Y. Hayne, saw in the situation what he took to be a chance to deliver a telling blow for his own discontented section. On the 19th of January he got the floor, and at the fag-end of a long day he held his colleagues' attention for an hour.

The thing that Hayne had in mind to do primarily was to draw the West to the side of the South, in common opposition to the East. He therefore

THE WEBSTER-HAYNE DEBATE

vigorously attacked the Foote resolution, agreeing with Benton that it was an expression of Eastern jealousy and that its adoption would greatly retard the development of the West. He laid much stress upon the common interests of the Western and Southern people and openly invited the one to an alliance with the other. He deprecated the tendencies of the Federal Government to consolidation and declared himself "opposed, in any shape, to all unnecessary extension of the powers or the influence of the Legislature or Executive of the Union over the States, or the people of the States." Throughout the speech ran side by side the twin ideas of strict construction and state rights; in every sentence breathed the protest of South Carolina against the protective tariff.

Just as the South Carolinian began speaking, a shadow darkened the doorway of the Senate chamber, and Daniel Webster stepped casually inside. The Massachusetts member was at the time absorbed in the preparation of certain cases that were coming up before the Supreme Court, and he had given little attention either to Foote's resolution or to the debate upon it. What he now heard, however, quickly drove Carver's Lessee *vs.* John Jacob Astor quite out of his mind. Aspersions were being cast upon his beloved New England; the Constitution was under attack; the Union itself was being called in question. Webster's decision was instantaneous: Hayne must be answered — and answered while his arguments were still hot.

"Seeing the true grounds of the Constitution thus attacked," the New Englander subsequently explained at a public dinner in New York, "I raised my voice in its favor, I must confess, with no preparation or previous intention. I can hardly say that I embarked in the contest from a sense of duty. It was an instantaneous impulse of inclination, not acting against duty, I trust, but hardly waiting for its suggestions. I felt it to be a contest for the integrity of the Constitution, and I was ready to enter into it, not thinking, or caring, personally, how I came out." In a speech characterized by Henry Cabot Lodge as "one of the most effective retorts, one of the strongest pieces of destructive criticism, ever uttered in the Senate," Webster now defended his section against the charges of selfishness, jealousy, and snobbishness that had been brought against it, and urged that the Senate and the people be made to hear no more utterances, such as those of Hayne, tending "to

THE WEBSTER-HAYNE DEBATE 147

bring the Union into discussion, as a mere question of present and temporary expediency."

The debate was now fairly started, and the word quickly went round that a battle of the giants was impending. Each foeman was worthy of the other's steel. Hayne was representative of all that was proudest and best in the South Carolina of his day. "Nature had lavished on him," says Benton, "all the gifts which lead to eminence in public, and to happiness in private, life." He was tall, well-proportioned, graceful; his features were clean-cut and expressive of both intelligence and amiability; his manner was cordial and unaffected; his mind was vigorous and his industry unremitting. Furthermore, he was an able lawyer, a fluent orator, a persuasive debater, an adroit parliamentarian. Upon entering the Senate at the early age of thirty-two, he had won prompt recognition by a powerful speech in opposition to the tariff of 1824; and by 1828, when he was reëlected, he was known as the South's ablest and boldest spokesman in the upper chamber.

Webster was an equally fitting representative of rugged New England. Born nine years earlier than Hayne, he struggled up from a boyhood of physical frailty and poverty to an honored place at the

Boston bar, and in 1812, at the age of thirty, was elected to Congress. To the Senate he brought, in 1827, qualities that gave him at once a preeminent position. His massive head, beetling brow, flashing eye, and stately carriage attracted instant attention wherever he went. His physical impressiveness was matched by lofty traits of character and by extraordinary powers of intellect; and by 1830 he had acquired a reputation for forensic ability and legal acumen which were second to none.

When, therefore, on the 21st of January, Hayne rose to deliver his *First Reply*, and Webster five days later took the floor to begin his *Second Reply* — probably the greatest effort in the history of American legislative oratory — the little chamber then used by the Senate, but nowadays given over to the Supreme Court, presented a spectacle fairly to be described as historic. Every senator who could possibly be present answered at roll call. Here were Webster's more notable fellow New Englanders — John Holmes of Maine, Levi Woodbury of New Hampshire, Horatio Seymour of Vermont. There were Mahlon Dickerson and Theodore Frelinghuysen of New Jersey, and John M. Clayton of Delaware. Here, John Tyler of Vir-

THE WEBSTER-HAYNE DEBATE 149

ginia, John Forsyth of Georgia, William R. King of Alabama; there, Hugh L. White and Felix Grundy of Tennessee, and Thomas H. Benton of Missouri. From the President's chair Hayne's distinguished fellow South Carolinian, Calhoun, looked down upon the assemblage with emotions which he vainly strove to conceal.

During the later stages of the discussion people of prominence from adjoining States filled the hotels of the city and bombarded the senators with requests for tickets of admission to the senate galleries. Lines were formed, and when the doors were thrown open in the morning every available inch of space was instantly filled with interested and excited spectators. So great was the pressure that all rules governing the admission of the public were waived. On the day of Webster's greatest effort ladies were admitted to the seats of the members, and the throng overflowed through the lobbies and down the long stairways, quite beyond hearing distance. In the House of Representatives the Speaker remained at his post, but the attendance was so scant that no business could be transacted.

Hayne's speech — begun on the 21st and continued on the 25th of January — was the fullest and

150 THE REIGN OF ANDREW JACKSON

most forceful exposition of the doctrines of strict construction, state rights, and nullification that had ever fallen upon the ear of Congress. It was no mere piece of abstract argumentation. Hayne was not the man to shrink from personalities, and he boldly accused the New England Federalists of disloyalty and Webster himself of complicity in "bargain and corruption." Thrusting and parrying, he stirred his supporters to wild enthusiasm and moved even the solemn-visaged Vice President to smiles of approval. The nationalists winced and wondered whether their champion would be able to measure up with so keen an antagonist. Webster sat staring into space, breaking his reverie only now and then to make a few notes.

The debate reached a climax in Webster's powerful *Second Reply*, on the 26th and 27th of January. Everything was favorable for a magnificent effort: the hearing was brilliant, the theme was vital, the speaker was in the prime of his matchless powers. On the desk before the New Englander as he arose were only five small letter-paper pages of notes. He spoke with such immediate preparation merely as the labors of a single evening made possible. But it may be doubted whether any forensic effort in our history was ever more thoroughly prepared

THE WEBSTER-HAYNE DEBATE 151

for, because Webster *lived* his speech before he spoke it. The origins of the Federal Union, the theories and applications of the Constitution, the history and bearings of nullification — these were matters with which years of study, observation, professional activity, and association with men had made him absolutely familiar. If any living American could answer Hayne and his fellow partizans, Webster was the man to do it.

Forty-eight in the total of seventy-three pages of print filled by this speech are taken up with a defense of New England against the Southern charges of sectionalism and disloyalty. Few utterances of the time are more familiar than the sentences bringing this part of the oration to a close: "Mr. President, I shall enter on no encomium of Massachusetts; she needs none. There she is. Behold her, and judge for yourselves. There is her history; the world knows it by heart. . . . There is Boston, and Concord, and Lexington, and Bunker Hill; and there they will remain forever." If this had been all, the speech would have been only a spirited defense of the good name of a section and would hardly have gained immortality. It was the Union, however, that most needed defense; and for that service the orator reserved his grandest efforts.

From the opening of the discussion Webster's object had been to "force from Hayne or his supporters a full, frank, clear-cut statement of what nullification meant; and then, by opposing to this doctrine the Constitution as he understood it, to show its utter inadequacy and fallaciousness either as constitutional law or as a practical working scheme."[1] In the Southerner's *First Reply* Webster found the statement that he wanted; he now proceeded to demolish it. Many pages of print would be required to reproduce, even in substance, the arguments which he employed. Yet the fundamentals are so simple that they can be stated in a dozen lines. Sovereignty, under our form of government, resides in the people of the United States. The exercise of the powers of sovereignty is entrusted by the people partly to the National Government and partly to the state Governments. This division of functions is made in the federal Constitution. If differences arise, as they must, as to the precise nature of the division, the decision rests — not with the state legislatures, as Hayne had said — but with the federal courts, which were established in part for that very purpose. No State has a right to "nullify" a federal law;

[1] MacDonald, *Jacksonian Democracy*, p. 98.

THE WEBSTER-HAYNE DEBATE 153

if one State has this right, all must have it, and the result can only be conflicts that would plunge the Government into chaos and the people ultimately into war. If the Constitution is not what the people want, they can amend it; but as long as it stands, the Constitution and all lawful government under it must be obeyed.

The incomparably eloquent peroration penetrated to the heart of the whole matter. The logic of nullification was disunion. Fine theories might be spun and dazzling phrases made to convince men otherwise, but the hard fact would remain. Hayne, Calhoun, and their like were playing with fire. Already they were boldly weighing "the chances of preserving liberty when the bonds that unite us together shall be broken asunder"; already they were hanging over the precipice of disunion, to see whether they could "fathom the depth of the abyss below." The last powerful words of the speech were, therefore, a glorification of the Union:

While the Union lasts, we have high, exciting, gratifying prospects spread out before us, for us and our children. Beyond that I seek not to penetrate the veil. God grant that in my day, at least, that curtain may not rise. . . . When my eyes shall be turned to behold for the last time the sun in heaven, may I not see him shining on the broken and dishonored fragments of a once glorious Union; on States dissevered, discordant, belligerent; on a land rent with civil feuds, or drenched, it may be, in fraternal blood! Let their last feeble and lingering glance, rather, behold the gorgeous ensign of the Republic, now known and honored throughout the earth, still full high advanced, its arms and trophies streaming in their original lustre, not a stripe erased or polluted, nor a single star obscured, bearing for its motto no such miserable interrogatory as "What is all this worth?" nor those other words of delusion and folly "Liberty first and Union afterward"; but everywhere, spread all over in characters of living light, blazing on all its ample folds, as they float over the sea and over the land, and in every wind under the whole heavens, that other sentiment, dear to every American heart — "Liberty *and* Union, now and forever, one and inseparable!"

Undaunted by the flood of eloquence that for four hours held the Senate spellbound, Hayne replied in a long speech that touched the zenith of his own masterful powers of argumentation. He conceded nothing. Each State, he still maintained, is "an independent sovereignty"; the Union is based upon a compact; and every party to the compact has a right to interpret for itself the terms of the agreement by which all are bound together. In a short, crisp speech, traversing the main ground which he had already gone over,

THE WEBSTER-HAYNE DEBATE 155

Webster exposed the inconsistencies and dangers involved in this argument; and the debate was over. The Foote resolution, long since forgotten, remained on the Senate calendar four months and was then tabled. Webster went back to his cases; the politicians turned again to their immediate concerns; the humdrum of congressional business was resumed; and popular interest drifted to other things.

Both sides were well satisfied with the presentation of their views. Certainly neither was converted to the position of the other. The debate served, however, to set before the country with greater clearness than ever before the two great systems of constitutional interpretation that were struggling for mastery, and large numbers of men whose ideas had been hazy were now led to adopt thoughtfully either the one body of opinions or the other. The country was not yet ready to follow the controversy to the end which Webster clearly foresaw — civil war. But each side treasured its vitalized and enriched arguments for use in a more strenuous day.

Advantage in the great discussion lay partly with Hayne and partly with his brilliant antagonist. On the whole, the facts of history were on the side of Hayne. Webster attempted to argue from the intent of the framers of the Constitution and from early opinion concerning the nature of the Union; but a careful appraisal of the evidence hardly bears out his contentions. On economic matters also, notably the operation of the protective tariff, he trod uncertain ground. He realized this fact and as far as possible kept clear of economic discussion. The South had real grievances, and Webster was well enough aware that they could not be argued out of existence.

On the other hand, the Northerner was vastly superior to his opponent in his handling of the theoretical issues of constitutional law; and in his exposition of the practical difficulties that would attend the operation of the principle of nullification he employed a fund of argument that was simply unanswerable. The logic of the larger phases of the situation lay, too, with him. If the Union for which he pleaded was not the Union which the Fathers intended to establish or even that which actually existed in the days of Washington and the elder Adams, it was at all events the Union in which, by the close of the fourth decade under the Constitution, a majority of the people of the United States had come to believe. It was the Union of Henry Clay, of Andrew Jackson, of Abraham Lincoln. And the largest significance of Webster's arguments in 1830 arises from the definiteness and force which they put into popular convictions that until then were vague and inarticulate — convictions which, as has been well said, "went on broadening and deepening until, thirty years afterward, they had a force sufficient to sustain the North and enable her to triumph in the terrible struggle which resulted in the preservation of national life." It was the *Second Reply* to Hayne which, more than any other single event or utterance between 1789 and 1860, "compacted the States into a nation."

CHAPTER VIII

TARIFF AND NULLIFICATION

IT was more than brilliant oratory that had drawn to the Senate chamber the distinguished audiences faced by Webster and Hayne in the great debate of 1830. The issues discussed touched the vitality and permanence of the nation itself. Nullification was no mere abstraction of the senator from South Carolina. It was a principle which his State — and, for aught one could tell, his section — was about to put into action. Already, in 1830, the air was tense with the coming controversy.

South Carolina had traveled a long road, politically, since 1789. In the days of Washington and the elder Adams the State was strongly Federalist. In 1800 Jefferson secured its electoral vote. But the Virginian's leadership was never fully accepted, and even before the Republican party had elsewhere submitted to the inevitable nationalization

TARIFF AND NULLIFICATION 159

the South Carolina membership was openly arrayed on the side of a protective tariff, the National Bank, and internal improvements. Calhoun and Cheves were for years among the most ardent exponents of broad constitutional construction; Hayne himself was elected to the Senate in 1822 as a nationalist, and over another candidate whose chief handicap was that he had proposed that his State secede rather than submit to the Missouri Compromise.

After 1824 sentiment rapidly shifted. The cause appeared to be the tariff; but in reality deeper forces were at work. South Carolina was an agricultural State devoted almost exclusively to the raising of cotton and rice. Soil and climate made her such, and the "peculiar institution" confirmed what Nature already had decreed. But the planters were now beginning to feel keenly the competition of the new cotton lands of the Gulf plains. As production increased, the price of cotton fell. "In 1816," writes Professor Turner, "the average price of middling uplands . . . was nearly thirty cents, and South Carolina's leaders favored the tariff; in 1820 it was seventeen cents, and the South saw in the protective system a grievance; in 1824 it was fourteen and three-quarters cents,

160 THE REIGN OF ANDREW JACKSON

and the South Carolinians denounced the tariff as unconstitutional."[1]

Men of the Clay-Adams school argued that the tariff stimulated industry, doubled the profits of agriculture, augmented wealth, and hence promoted the well-being of the nation as a whole. The Southern planter was never able to discover in the protective system any real advantage for himself, but as long as the tariffs were moderate he was influenced by nationalistic sentiment to accept them. The demand for protection on the part of the Northern manufacturers seemed, however, insatiable. An act of 1824 raised the duties on cotton and woolen goods. A measure of 1827 which applied to woolens the ruinous principle already applied to cottons was passed by the House and was laid on the table in the Senate only by the casting vote of Vice President Calhoun. The climax was reached in the Tariff Act of 1828, which the Southerners themselves loaded with objectionable provisions in the vain hope of making it so abominable that even New England congressmen would vote against it.

A few years of such legislation sufficed to rouse the South to a deep feeling of grievance. It was no

[1] Turner, *The Rise of the New West*, p. 325.

TARIFF AND NULLIFICATION 161

longer a question of reasonable concession to the general national good. A vast artificial economic system had been set up, whose benefits accrued to the North and whose burdens fell disproportionately upon the South. The tone and temper of the manufacturing sections and of the agricultural West gave no promise of a change of policy. The obvious conclusion was that the planting interests must find some means of bringing pressure to bear for their own relief.

The means which they found was nullification; and it fell to South Carolina, whose people were most ardent in their resentment of anything that looked like discrimination, to put the remedy to the test. The Legislature of this State had made an early beginning by denouncing the tariff of 1824 as unconstitutional. In 1827 Robert J. Turnbull, one of the abler political leaders, published under the title of *The Crisis* a series of essays in which he boldly proclaimed nullification as the remedy. In the following summer Calhoun put the nullification doctrine into its first systematic form in a paper — the so-called *Exposition* — which for some time was known to the public only as the report of a committee of the Legislature.

By 1829 the State was sharply divided into two

162 THE REIGN OF ANDREW JACKSON

parties, the nationalists and the nullifiers. All were agreed that the protective system was iniquitous and that it must be broken down. The difference was merely as to method. The nationalists favored working through the customary channels of legislative reform; the nullifiers urged that the State interpose its authority to prevent the enforcement of the objectionable laws. For a time the leaders wavered. But the swing of public sentiment in the direction of nullification was rapid and overwhelming, and one by one the representatives in Congress and other men of prominence fell into line. Hayne and McDuffie were among the first to give it their support; and Calhoun, while he was for a time held back by his political aspirations and by his obligations as Vice President, came gradually to feel that his political future would be worth little unless he had the support of his own State.

As the election of 1828 approached, the hope of the discontented forces centered in Jackson. They did not overlook the fact that his record was that of a moderate protectionist. But the same was true of many South Carolinians and Georgians, and it seemed not at all impossible that, as a Southern man and a cotton planter, he should

TARIFF AND NULLIFICATION 163

undergo a change of heart no less decisive than that which Hayne and Calhoun had experienced. Efforts to draw him out, however, proved not very successful. Lewis saw to it that Jackson's utterances while yet he was a candidate were safely colorless; and the single mention of the tariff contained in the inaugural address was susceptible of the most varied interpretations. The annual message of 1829 indicated opposition to protection; on the other hand, the presidential message of the next year not only asserted the full power of Congress to levy protective duties but declared the abandonment of protection "neither to be expected or desired." Gradually the antiprotectionist leaders were made to see that the tariff was not a subject upon which the President felt keenly, and that therefore it was useless to look to him for effective support.

Even the adroit efforts which were made to get from the incoming executive expressions that could be interpreted as endorsements of nullification were successfully fended off. For some months the President gave no outward sign of his disapproval. With more than his usual deliberateness, Jackson studied the situation, awaiting the right moment to speak out with the maximum of effect.

164 THE REIGN OF ANDREW JACKSON

The occasion finally came on April 13, 1830, at a banquet held in Washington in celebration of Jefferson's birthday. The Virginia patron of democracy had been dead four years, and Jackson had become, more truly than any other man, his successor. Jacksonian democracy was, however, something very different from Jeffersonian, and never was the contrast more evident than on this fateful evening. During the earlier part of the festivities a series of prearranged toasts, accompanied by short speeches, put before the assemblage the Jeffersonian teachings in a light highly favorable — doubtless unwarrantably so — to the ultra state rights theory. Then followed a number of volunteer toasts. The President was, of course, accorded the honor of proposing the first — and this gave Jackson his chance. Rising in his place and drawing himself up to his full height, he raised his right hand, looked straight at Calhoun and, amid breathless silence, exclaimed in that crisp, harsh tone that had so often been heard above the crashing of many rifles: "Our Union! It must be preserved!"

An account of the scene which is given by Isaac Hill, a member of the Kitchen Cabinet and an eyewitness, is interesting:

TARIFF AND NULLIFICATION 165

A proclamation of martial law in South Carolina and an order to arrest Calhoun where he sat could not have come with more blinding, staggering force. All hilarity ceased. The President, without adding one word in the way of speech, lifted up his glass as a notice that the toast was to be quaffed standing. Calhoun rose with the rest. His glass so trembled in his hand that a little of the amber fluid trickled down the side. Jackson stood silent and impassive. There was no response to the toast. Calhoun waited until all sat down. Then he slowly and with hesitating accent offered the second volunteer toast: "The Union! Next to Our Liberty Most Dear!" Then, after a minute's hesitation, and in a way that left doubt as to whether he intended it for part of the toast or for the preface to a speech, he added: "May we all remember that it can only be preserved by respecting the rights of the States and by distributing equally the benefit and burden of the Union."

The nullifiers had carefully planned the evening's proceedings with a purpose to strengthen their cause with the country. They had not reckoned on the President, and the dash of cold water which he had administered caused them more anguish than any opposition that they had yet encountered. The banquet broke up earlier than had been expected, and the diners went off by twos and threes in eager discussion of the scene that they had witnessed. Some were livid with rage; some shook their heads in fear of civil war; but most

166 THE REIGN OF ANDREW JACKSON

rejoiced in the splendid exhibition of executive dignity and patriotic fervor which the President had given. Subsequently it transpired that Jackson had acted on no mere impulse and that his course had been carefully planned in consultation with Van Buren and other advisers.

Throughout the summer and autumn of 1830 both the State Rights and Union parties in South Carolina worked feverishly to perfect their organizations. The issue that both were making ready to meet was nothing less than the election of a convention to nullify the tariff laws. Those upholding nullification lost no opportunity to consolidate their forces, and by the close of the year these were clearly in the majority, although the unionist element contained many of the ablest and most respected men in the State. Calhoun directed the nullifier campaign, though he did not throw off all disguises until the summer of the following year.

Though Jackson made no further public declarations, the views which he expressed in private were usually not slow to reach the public ear. In a letter to a committee of the Union party in response to an invitation to attend a Fourth of July dinner the President intimated that force might properly be employed if nullification should be attempted. And to a South Carolina Congressman who was setting off on a trip home he said: "Tell them [the nullifiers] from me that they can talk and write resolutions and print threats to their hearts' content. But if one drop of blood be shed there in defiance of the laws of the United States, I will hang the first man of them I can get my hands on to the first tree I can find." When Hayne heard of this threat he expressed in Benton's hearing a doubt as to whether the President would really hang anybody. "I tell you, Hayne," the Missourian replied, "when Jackson begins to talk about hanging, they can begin to look for the ropes."

Meanwhile actual nullification awaited the decision of the Vice President to surrender himself completely to the cause and to become its avowed leader. Calhoun did not find this an easy decision to make. Above all things he wanted to be President. He was not the author of nullification; and although he did not fully realize until too late how much his state rights leanings would cost him in the North, he was shrewd enough to know that his political fortunes would not be bettered by his becoming involved in a great sectional controversy. Circumstances worked together, however, to force

Calhoun gradually into the position of chief prominence in the dissenting movement. The tide of public opinion in his State swept him along with it; the breach with Jackson severed the last tie with the northern and western democracy; and his resentment of Van Buren's rise to favor prompted words and acts which completed the isolation of the South Carolinian. His party's enthusiastic acceptance of Jackson as a candidate for reëlection in 1832 and of "Little Van" as a candidate for the vice presidency — and, by all tokens, for the presidency four years later — was the last straw. Broken and desperate, Calhoun sank back into the rôle of an extremist, sectional leader. There was no need of further concealment; and in midsummer, 1831, he issued his famous *Address to the People of South Carolina*, and this restatement of the *Exposition* of 1828 now became the avowed platform of the nullification party. The *Fort Hill Letter* of August 28, 1832, addressed to Governor Hamilton, was a simpler and clearer presentation of the same body of doctrine.

Matters were at last brought to a head by a new piece of tariff legislation which was passed in 1832 not to appease South Carolina but to take advantage of a comfortable state of affairs that had arisen

TARIFF AND NULLIFICATION 169

in the national treasury. The public lands were again selling well, and the late tariff laws were yielding lavishly. The national debt was dwindling to the point of disappearance, and the country had more money than it could use. Jackson therefore called upon Congress to revise the tariff system so as to reduce the revenue, and in the session of 1831-32 several bills to that end were brought forward. The scale of duties finally embodied in the Act of July 14, 1832, corrected many of the anomalies of the Act of 1828, but it cut off some millions of revenue without making any substantial change in the protective system. Virginia and North Carolina voted heavily for the bill, but South Carolina and Georgia as vigorously opposed it; and the nullifiers refused to see in it any concession to the tariff principles for which they stood. "I no longer consider the question one of free trade," wrote Calhoun when the passage of the bill was assured, "but of consolidation." In an address to their constituents the South Carolina delegation in Congress declared that "protection must now be regarded as the settled policy of the country," that "all hope from Congress is irrevocably gone," and that it was for the people to decide "whether the rights and liberties which you received as a

170   THE REIGN OF ANDREW JACKSON

precious inheritance from an illustrious ancestry shall be tamely surrendered without a struggle, or transmitted undiminished to your posterity."

In the disaffected State events now moved rapidly. The elections of the early autumn were carried by the nullifiers, and the new Legislature, acting on the recommendation of Governor Hamilton, promptly called a state convention to consider whether the "federal compact" had been violated and what remedy should be adopted. The 162 delegates who gathered at Columbia on the 19th of November were, socially and politically, the élite of the State: Hamiltons, Haynes, Pinckneys, Butlers — almost all of the great families of a State of great families were represented. From the outset the convention was practically of one mind; and an ordinance of nullification drawn up by a committee of twenty-one was adopted within five days by a vote of 136 to 26.

The tariff acts of 1828 and 1832 were declared "null, void, and no law, nor binding upon this State, its officers or citizens." None of the duties in question were to be permitted to be collected in the State after February 1, 1833. Appeals to the federal courts for enforcement of the invalidated

TARIFF AND NULLIFICATION 171

acts were forbidden, and all officeholders, except members of the Legislature, were required to take an oath to uphold the ordinance. Calhoun had laboriously argued that nullification did not mean disunion. But his contention was not sustained by the words of the ordinance, which stated unequivocally that the people of the State would not "submit to the application of force on the part of the federal Government to reduce this State to obedience." Should force be used, the ordinance boldly declared — indeed, should *any* action contrary to the will of the people be taken to execute the measures declared void — such efforts would be regarded as "inconsistent with the longer continuance of South Carolina in the Union," and "the people of this State" would "thenceforth hold themselves absolved from all further obligation to maintain or preserve their political connection with the people of the other States, and will forthwith proceed to organize a separate Government, and to do all other acts and things which sovereign and independent States may of right do."

In accordance with the instructions of the convention, the Legislature forthwith reassembled to pass the measures deemed necessary to enforce the ordinance. A replevin act provided for the recovery of goods seized or detained for payment of duty; the use of military force, including volunteers, to "repel invasion" was authorized; and provision was made for the purchase of arms and ammunition. Throughout the State a martial tone resounded. Threats of secession and war were heard on every side. Nightly meetings were held and demonstrations were organized. Blue cockades with a palmetto button in the center became the most popular of ornaments. Medals were struck bearing the inscription: "John C. Calhoun, First President of the Southern Confederacy." The Legislature, reassembling in December, elected Hayne as Governor and chose Calhoun — who now resigned the vice presidency — to take the vacant seat in the Senate. In his first message to the Legislature Webster's former antagonist declared his purpose to carry into full effect the nullification ordinance and the legislation supplementary to it, and expressed confidence that, if the sacred soil of the State should be "polluted by the footsteps of an invader," no one of her sons would be found "raising a parricidal arm against our common mother."

Thus the proud commonwealth was panoplied for a contest of wits, and perchance of arms, with

TARIFF AND NULLIFICATION 173

the nation. Could it hope to win? South Carolina had a case which had been forcibly and plausibly presented. It could count on a deep reluctance of men in every part of the country to see the nation fall into actual domestic combat. There were, however, a dozen reasons why victory could not reasonably be looked for. One would have been enough — the presence of Andrew Jackson in the White House.

Through federal officers and the leaders of the Union party Jackson kept himself fully informed upon the situation, and six weeks before the nullification convention was called he began preparations to meet all eventualities. The naval authorities at Norfolk were directed to be in readiness to dispatch a squadron to Charleston; the commanders of the forts in Charleston Harbor were ordered to double their vigilance and to defend their posts against any persons whatsoever; troops were ordered from Fortress Monroe; and General Scott was sent to take full command and to strengthen the defenses as he found necessary. The South Carolinians were to be allowed to talk, and even to adopt "ordinances," to their hearts' content. But the moment they stepped across the line of disobedience to the laws of the United States they

174 THE REIGN OF ANDREW JACKSON

were to be made to feel the weight of the nation's restraining hand.

"The duty of the Executive is a plain one," wrote the President to Joel R. Poinsett, a prominent South Carolina unionist; "the laws will be executed and the United States preserved by all the constitutional and legal means he is invested with." When the situation bore its most serious aspect Jackson received a call from Sam Dale, who had been one of his dispatch bearers at the Battle of New Orleans. "General Dale," exclaimed the President during the conversation, "if this thing goes on, our country will be like a bag of meal with both ends open. Pick it up in the middle or endwise, and it will run out. I must tie the bag and save the country." "Dale," he exclaimed again later, "they are trying me here; you will witness it; but, by the God of heaven, I will uphold the laws." "I understood him to be referring to nullification again," related Dale in his account of the interview, "and I expressed the hope that things would go right." "They *shall* go right, sir," the President fairly shouted, shattering his pipe on the table by way of further emphasis.

When Jackson heard that the convention at Columbia had taken the step expected of it, he

TARIFF AND NULLIFICATION 175

made the following entry in his diary: "South Carolina has passed her ordinance of nullification and secession. As soon as it can be had in authentic form, meet it with a proclamation." The proclamation was issued December 10, 1832. Parton relates that the President wrote the first draft of this proclamation under such a glow of feeling that he was obliged "to scatter the written pages all over the table to let them dry," and that the document was afterwards revised by his scholarly Secretary of State, Edward Livingston. With Jackson supplying the ideas and spirit and Livingston the literary form, the result was the ablest and most impressive state paper of the period. It categorically denied the right of a State either to annul a federal law or to secede from the Union. It admitted that the laws complained of operated unequally but took the position that this must be true of all revenue measures. It expressed the inflexible determination of the Administration to repress and punish every form of resistance to federal authority. Deep argument, solemn warning, and fervent entreaty were skillfully combined. But the most powerful effect was likely to be that produced by the President's flaming denial — set in bold type in the contemporary prints — of the

Hayne-Calhoun creed: "I consider the power to annul a law of the United States, assumed by one State, incompatible with the existence of the Union, contradicted expressly by the letter of the Constitution, unauthorized by its spirit, inconsistent with every principle on which it was founded, and destructive of the great object for which it was formed."

Throughout the North this vindication of national dignity and power struck a responsive chord, and for once even the Adams and Clay men found themselves in hearty agreement with the President. Bostonians gathered in Faneuil Hall and New Yorkers in a great meeting in the Park to shower encomiums upon the proclamation and upon its author. The nullifiers did not at once recoil from the blow. The South Carolina Legislature called upon Governor Hayne officially to warn "the good people of this State against the attempt of the President of the United States to seduce them from their allegiance"; and the resulting counterblast, in the form of a proclamation made public on the 20th of December, was as vigorous as the liveliest "fire-eater" could have wished. The Governor declared that the State would maintain its sovereignty or be "buried beneath its ruins."

TARIFF AND NULLIFICATION 177

The date of the expected crisis — February 1, 1833, when the nullification ordinance was to take effect — was now near at hand, and on both sides preparations were pushed. During the interval, however, the tide turned decidedly against the nullifiers. A call for a general convention of the States "to determine and consider . . . questions of disputed power" served only to draw out strong expressions of disapproval of the South Carolina program, showing that it could not expect even moral support from outside. On the 16th of January Jackson asked Congress for authority to alter or abolish certain ports of entry, to use force to execute the revenue laws, and to try in the federal courts cases that might arise from the present emergency. Five days later a bill on these lines — popularly denominated the "Force Bill" — was introduced; and while many men who had no sympathy with nullification drew back from a plan involving the coercion of a State, it was soon settled that some sort of measure for strengthening the President's hand would be passed.

Meanwhile a way of escape from the whole difficulty was unexpectedly opened. The friends of Van Buren began to fear that the disagreement of North and South upon the tariff question would

178 THE REIGN OF ANDREW JACKSON

cost their favorite the united support of the party in 1836. Accordingly they set on foot a movement in Congress to bring about a moderate reduction of the prevailing rates; and it was of course their hope that the nullifiers would be induced to recede altogether from the position which they had taken. Through Verplanck of New York, the Ways and Means Committee of the House brought in a measure reducing the duties, within two years, to about half the existing rates. Jackson approved the plan, although personally he had little to do with it.

But though the Verplanck Bill could not muster sufficient support to become law, it revived tariff discussion on promising lines, and it brought nullification proceedings to a halt in the very nick of time. Shortly before February 1, 1833, the leading nullifiers came together in Charleston and entered into an extralegal agreement to postpone the enforcement of the nullification ordinance until the outcome of the new tariff debates should be known. The failure of the Verplanck measure, however, left matters where they were, and civil war in South Carolina again loomed ominously.

In this juncture patriots of all parties turned to the one man whose leadership seemed indispensable

TARIFF AND NULLIFICATION 179

in tariff legislation — the "great pacificator," Henry Clay, who after two years in private life had just taken his seat in the Senate. Clay was no friend of Jackson or of Van Buren, and it required much sacrifice of personal feeling to lend his services to a program whose political benefits would almost certainly accrue to his rivals. Finally, however, he yielded and on the 12th of February he rose in the Senate and offered a compromise measure proposing that on all articles which paid more than twenty per cent the amount in excess of that rate should be reduced by stages until in 1842 it would entirely disappear.

Stormy debates followed on both the Compromise Tariff and the Force Bill, but before the session closed on the 4th of March both were on the statute book. When, therefore, the South Carolina convention, in accordance with an earlier proclamation of Governor Hamilton, reassembled on the 11th of March, the wind had been taken out of the nullifiers' sails; the laws which they had "nullified" had been repealed, and there was nothing for the convention to do but to rescind the late ordinance and the legislative measures supplementary to it. There was a chance, however, for one final fling. By a vote of 132 to 19 the convention soberly adopted an ordinance nullifying the Force Bill and calling on the Legislature to pass laws to prevent the execution of that measure — which, indeed, nobody was now proposing to execute.

So the tempest passed. Both sides claimed victory, and with some show of reason. So far as was possible without an actual test of strength, the authority of the Federal Government had been vindicated and its dignity maintained; the constitutional doctrines of Webster acquired a new sanction; the fundamental point was enforced that a law — that *every* law — enacted by Congress must be obeyed until repealed or until set aside by the courts as unconstitutional. On the other hand, the nullifiers had brought about the repeal of the laws to which they objected and had been largely instrumental in turning the tariff policy of the country for some decades into a new channel. Moreover they expressed no regret for their acts and in no degree renounced the views upon which those acts had been based. They submitted to the authority of the United States, but on terms fixed by themselves. And, what is more, they supplied practically every constitutional and political argument to be used by their sons in 1860 to justify secession.

CHAPTER IX

THE WAR ON THE UNITED STATES BANK

"NOTHING lacks now to complete the love-feast," wrote Isaac Hill sardonically to Thomas H. Benton after the collapse of nullification, "but for Jackson and Webster to solemnize the coalition [in support of the Union] with a few mint-juleps! I think I could arrange it, if assured of the coöperation of yourself and Blair on our side, and Jerry Mason and Nick Biddle on theirs. But never fear, my friend. This mixing of oil and water is only the temporary shake-up of Nullification. Wait till Jackson gets at the Bank again, and then the scalping-knives will glisten once more."

The South Carolina controversy had indeed brought Jacksonians and anti-Jacksonians together. But once the tension was relaxed, there began the conflict of interests which the New Hampshire editor had predicted. Men fell again into their customary political relationships; issues that for the

182 THE REIGN OF ANDREW JACKSON

moment had been pushed into the background — internal improvements, public land policy, distribution of surplus revenue, and above all the Bank — were revived in full vigor. Now, indeed, the President entered upon the greatest task to which he had yet put his hand. To curb nullification was a worthy achievement. But, after all, Congress and an essentially united nation had stood firmly behind the Executive at every stage of that performance. To destroy the United States Bank was a different matter, for this institution had the full support of one of the two great parties in which the people of the country were now grouped; Jackson's own party was by no means a unit in opposing it; and the prestige and influence of the Bank were such as to enable it to make a powerful fight against any attempts to annihilate it.

The second Bank of the United States was chartered in 1816 for twenty years, with a capital of thirty-five million dollars, one-fifth of which had been subscribed by the Government. For some time it was not notably successful, partly because of bad management but mainly because of the disturbance of business which the panic of 1819 had produced. Furthermore, its power over local

THE UNITED STATES BANK 183

banks and over the currency system made it unpopular in the West and South, and certain States sought to cripple it by taxing out of existence the several branches which the board of directors voted to establish. In two notable decisions — M'Culloch *vs.* Maryland in 1819 and Osborn *vs.* United States Bank in 1824 — the Supreme Court saved the institution by denying the power of a State to impose taxation of the sort and by asserting unequivocally the right of Congress to enact the legislation upon which the Bank rested. And after Nicholas Biddle, a Philadelphia lawyer-diplomat, succeeded Langdon Cheves as president of the Bank in 1823 an era of great prosperity set in.

The forces of opposition were never reconciled; indeed, every evidence of the increasing strength of the Bank roused them to fresh hostility. The verdict of the Supreme Court in support of the constitutionality of the Act of 1816 carried conviction to few people who were not already convinced. The restraints which the Bank imposed upon the dubious operations of the southern and western banks were vigorously resented. The Bank was regarded as a great financial monopoly, an "octopus," and Biddle as an autocrat bent only on dominating the entire banking and currency system of the country.

On Jackson's attitude toward the Bank before he became President we have little direct information. But it is sufficiently clear that eventually he came to share the hostile views of his Tennessee friends and neighbors. In 1817 he refused to sign a memorial "got up by the aristocracy of Nashville" for the establishment of a branch in that town. When, ten years later, such a branch was installed, General Thomas Cadwalader of Philadelphia, agent of the Bank, visited the town to supervise the arrangements and became very friendly with the "lord of the Hermitage." But correspondence of succeeding years, though filled with insinuating cordiality, failed to bring out any expression of goodwill toward the institution such as the agent manifestly coveted.

Jackson seems to have carried to Washington in 1829 a deep distrust of the Bank, and he was disposed to speak out boldly against it in his inaugural address. But he was persuaded by his friends that this would be ill-advised, and he therefore made no mention of the subject. Yet he made no effort to conceal his attitude, for he wrote to Biddle a few months after the inauguration that he did

THE UNITED STATES BANK 185

not believe that Congress had power to charter a bank outside of the District of Columbia, that he did not dislike the United States Bank more than other banks, but that ever since he had read the history of the South Sea Bubble he had been afraid of banks. After this confession the writer hardly needed to confess that he was "no economist, no financier."

Most of the officers of the "mother bank" at Philadelphia and of the branches were anti-Jackson men, and Jackson's friends put the idea into his mind that the Bank had used its influence against him in the late campaign. Specific charges of partizanship were brought against Jeremiah Mason, president of the branch at Portsmouth, New Hampshire; and although an investigation showed the accusation to be groundless, Biddle's heated defense of the branch had no effect save to rouse the Jacksonians to a firmer determination to compass the downfall of the Bank.

Biddle labored manfully to stem the tide. He tried to improve his personal relations with the President, and he even allowed Jackson men to gain control of several of the western branches. The effort, however, was in vain. When he thought the situation right, Biddle brought forward a plan for a new charter which received the assent of most of the members of the official Cabinet, as well as that of some of the "Kitchen" group. But Jackson met the proposal with his unshakable constitutional objections and, to Biddle's deep disappointment, advanced in his first annual message to the formal, public assault. The Bank's charter, he reminded Congress, would expire in 1836; request for a new charter would probably soon be forthcoming; the matter could not receive too early attention from the legislative branch. "Both the constitutionality and the expediency of the law creating this bank," declared the President, "are well questioned by a large portion of our fellow-citizens; and it must be admitted by all that it has failed in the great end of establishing a uniform and sound currency." The first part of the statement was true, but the second was distinctly unfair. The Bank, to be sure, had not established "a uniform and sound" currency. But it had accomplished much toward that end and was practically the only agency that was wielding any influence in that direction. The truth is that the more efficient the Bank proved in this task the less popular it became among those elements of the people from which Jackson mainly drew his strength.

THE UNITED STATES BANK 187

Nothing came of the President's admonition except committee reports in the two Houses, both favorable to the Bank; in fact, the Senate report was copied almost verbatim from a statement supplied by Biddle. A year later Jackson returned to the subject, this time with an alternative plan for a national bank to be organized as a branch of the Treasury and hence to have "no means to operate on the hopes, fears, or interests of large masses of the community." In a set of autograph notes from which the second message was prepared the existing Bank was declared not only unconstitutional but dangerous to liberty, "because through its officers, loans, and participation in politics it could build up or pull down parties or men, because it created a monopoly of the money power, because much of the stock was owned by foreigners, because it would always support him who supported it, and because it weakened the state and strengthened the general government." Congress paid no attention to either criticisms or recommendations, and the supporters of the Bank took fresh heart.

When Congress again met, in December, 1831, a presidential election was impending and everybody was wondering what part the bank question would

188 THE REIGN OF ANDREW JACKSON

play. Most Democrats were of the opinion that the subject should be kept in the background. After all, the present bank charter had more than four years to run, and there seemed to be no reason for injecting so thorny an issue into the campaign. With a view to keeping the bank authorities quiet, two members of the reconstructed Cabinet, Livingston and McLane, entered into a *modus vivendi* with Biddle under which the Administration agreed not to push the issue until after the election. In his annual report as Secretary of the Treasury, McLane actually made an argument for rechartering the Bank; and in his message of the 6th of December the President said that, while he still held "the opinions heretofore expressed in relation to the Bank as at present organized," he would "leave it for the present to the investigation of an enlightened people and their representatives." He had been persuaded that his own plan for a Bank, suggested a year earlier, was not feasible.

Biddle now made a supreme mistake. Misled in some degree unquestionably by the optimistic McLane, he got the idea that Jackson was weakening, that the Democrats were afraid to take a stand on the subject until after the election, and that now was the strategic time to strike for a new

THE UNITED STATES BANK 189

charter. In this belief he was further encouraged by Clay, Webster, and other leading anti-Administration men, as well as by McDuffie, a Calhoun supporter and chairman of the Ways and Means Committee of the House. There was small doubt that a bill for a new charter could be carried in both branches of Congress. Jackson must either sign it, argued Biddle's advisers, or run grave risk of losing Pennsylvania and other commercial States whose support was necessary to his election. On the other hand, Biddle was repeatedly warned that an act for a new charter would be vetoed. He chose to press the issue and on January 9, 1832, the formal application of the Bank for a renewal of its charter was presented to Congress, and within a few weeks bills to recharter were reported in both Houses.

Realizing that defeat or even a slender victory in Congress would be fatal, the Bank flooded Washington with lobbyists, and Biddle himself appeared upon the scene to lead the fight. The measure was carried by safe majorities — in the Senate, on the 11th of June, by a vote of 28 to 20, and in the House on the 3d of July, by a vote of 107 to 86. To the dismay of the bank forces, although it ought not to have been to their surprise,

190 THE REIGN OF ANDREW JACKSON

Jackson was as good as his word. On the 10th of July the bill was vetoed. The veto message as transmitted to the Senate was probably written by Taney, but the ideas were Jackson's — ideas which, so far as they relate to finance and banking operations, have been properly characterized as "in the main beneath contempt." The message, however, was intended as a campaign document, and as such it showed great ingenuity. It attacked the Bank as a monopoly, a "hydra of corruption," and an instrumentality of federal encroachment on the rights of the States, and in a score of ways appealed to the popular distrust of capitalistic institutions. The message acquired importance, too, from the President's extraordinary claim to the right of judging both the constitutionality and the expediency of proposed legislation, independently of Congress and the Courts.

The veto plunged the Senate into days of acrid debate. Clay pronounced Jackson's construction of the veto power "irreconcilable with the genius of representative government." Webster declared that responsibility for the ruin of the Bank and for the disasters that might follow would have to be borne by the President alone. Benton and other prominent members, however, painted Jackson as

THE UNITED STATES BANK 191

the savior of his country; and the second vote of 22 to 19 yielded a narrower majority for the bill than the first had done. Thus the measure perished.

The bank men received the veto with equanimity. They professed to believe that the balderdash in which the message abounded would make converts for their side; they even printed thirty thousand copies of the document for circulation. Events, however, did not sustain their optimism. In the ensuing campaign the Bank became, by its own choice, the leading issue. The National Republicans, whose nominee was Clay, defended the institution and attacked the veto; the Jacksonians reiterated on the stump every charge and argument that their leader had taught them. The verdict was decisive. Jackson received 219 and Clay 49 electoral votes.

The President was unquestionably right in interpreting his triumph as an endorsement of the veto, and he naturally felt that the question was settled. The officers and friends of the Bank still hoped, however, to snatch victory from defeat. They had no expectation of converting Jackson or of carrying a charter measure at an early date. But they foresaw that to wind up the business of the

Bank in 1836 it would be necessary to call in loans and to withdraw a vast amount of currency from circulation, with the result of a general disturbance, if not a severe crippling, of business. This, they thought, would bring about an eleventh-hour measure giving the Bank a new lease of life.

Jackson, too, realized that a sudden termination of the activities of the Bank would derange business and produce distress, and that under these circumstances a charter might be wrung from Congress in spite of a veto. But he had no intention of allowing matters to come to such a pass. His plan was rather to cut off by degrees the activities of the Bank, until at last they could be suspended altogether without a shock. The most obvious means of doing this was to withdraw the heavy deposits made by the Government; and to this course the President fully committed himself as soon as the results of the election were known. He was impelled, further, by the conviction — notwithstanding unimpeachable evidence to the contrary — that the Bank was insolvent, and by his indignation at the refusal of Biddle and his associates to accept the electoral verdict as final. "Biddle shan't have the public money to break down the public administration with. It's settled.

THE UNITED STATES BANK 193

My mind's made up." So the President declared to Blair early in 1833. And no one could have any reasonable doubt that decisive action would follow threat.

It was not, however, all plain sailing. Under the terms of the charter of 1816 public funds were to be deposited in the Bank and its branches unless the Secretary of the Treasury should direct that they be placed elsewhere; and such deposits elsewhere, together with actual withdrawals, were to be reported to Congress, with reasons for such action. McLane, the Secretary of the Treasury, was friendly toward the Bank and could not be expected to give the necessary orders for removal. This meant that the first step was to get a new head for the Treasury. But McLane was too influential a man to be summarily dismissed. Hence it was arranged that Livingston should become Minister to France and that McLane should succeed him as Secretary of State.

The choice of the new Secretary of the Treasury would have been a clever stroke if things had worked out as Jackson expected. The appointee was William J. Duane, son of the editor of the *Aurora*, which had long been the most popular and influential newspaper in Pennsylvania. This State

194 THE REIGN OF ANDREW JACKSON

was the seat of the "mother bank" and, although a Jackson stronghold, a cordial supporter of the proscribed institution; so that it was well worth while to forestall criticism in that quarter, so far as might be, by having the order for removal issued by a Pennsylvanian. Duane, however, accepted the post rather because he coveted office than because he supported the policy of removal, and when the test came Jackson found to his chagrin that he still had a Secretary who would not take the desired action. There was nothing to do but procure another; and this time he made no mistake. Duane, weakly protesting, was dismissed, and Roger B. Taney, the Attorney-General, was appointed in his stead. "I am fully prepared to go with you firmly through this business," Jackson was assured by the new Secretary, "and to meet all its consequences."

The way was now clear, and an order was issued requiring all treasury receipts after October 1, 1833, to be deposited in the Girard Bank of Philadelphia and twenty-two other designated state banks. Deposits in the United States Bank and its branches were not immediately "removed"; they were left, rather, to be withdrawn as the money was actually needed. Nevertheless there

THE UNITED STATES BANK 195

was considerable disturbance of business, and deputation after deputation came to the White House to ask that Taney's order be rescinded. Jackson, however, was sure that most of the trouble was caused by Biddle and his associates, and to all these appeals he remained absolutely deaf. After a time he refused so much as to see the petitioners. In his message of the 3d of December he assumed full responsibility for the removals, defending his course mainly on the ground that the Bank had been "actively engaged in attempting to influence the elections of the public officers by means of its money."

From this point the question became entirely one of politics. The Bank itself was doomed. On the one side, the National Republicans united in the position that the Administration had been entirely in the wrong, and that the welfare of the country demanded a great fiscal institution of the character of the Bank. On the other side, the Democrats, deriving, indeed, a new degree of unity from the controversy on this issue, upheld the President's every word and act. "You may continue," said Benton to his fellow partizans in the Senate, "to be for a bank and for Jackson, but you cannot be for this Bank and Jackson." Firmly

196 THE REIGN OF ANDREW JACKSON

allied with the Bank interests, the National Republicans resolved to bring all possible discomfiture upon the Administration.

The House of Representatives was controlled by the Democrats, and little could be accomplished there. But the Senate contained not only the three ablest anti-Jacksonians of the day — Clay, Webster, Calhoun — but an absolute majority of anti-Administration men; and there the attack was launched. On December 26, 1833, Clay introduced two resolutions declaring that in the removal of the deposits the President had "assumed upon himself authority and power not conferred by the Constitution and laws but in derogation of both," and pronouncing Taney's statement of reasons "unsatisfactory and insufficient." After a stormy debate, both resolutions in slightly amended form were carried by substantial majorities.

Jackson was not in the habit of meekly swallowing censure, and on the 15th of April he sent to the Senate a formal protest, characterizing the action of the body as "unauthorized by the Constitution, contrary to its spirit and to several of its express provisions," and "subversive of that distribution of the powers of government which it has ordained and established." Aside from a general defense of

THE UNITED STATES BANK 197

his course, the chief point that the President made was that the Constitution provided a procedure in cases of this kind, namely impeachment, which alone could be properly resorted to if the legislative branch desired to bring charges against the Executive. The Senate was asked respectfully to spread the protest on its records. This, however, it refused to do. On the contrary, it voted that the right of protest could not be recognized; and it found additional satisfaction in negativing an unusual number of the President's nominations.

Throughout the remainder of his second Administration Jackson maintained his hold upon the country and kept firm control in the lower branch of Congress. Until very near the end, the Senate, however, continued hostile. During the debate on the protest Benton served notice that he would introduce, at each succeeding session, a motion to expunge the resolution of censure. Such a motion was made in 1835, and again in 1836, without result. But at last, in January, 1837, after a debate lasting thirteen hours, the Senate adopted, by a vote of 24 to 19, a resolution meeting the Jacksonian demand.

The manuscript journal of the session of 1833–1834 was brought into the Senate, and the secretary, in obedience

198 THE REIGN OF ANDREW JACKSON

to the resolution, drew black lines around the resolution of censure, and wrote across the face thereof, "in strong letters," the words: "Expunged by order of the Senate, this sixteenth day of January, in the year of our Lord 1837." Many members withdrew rather than witness the proceeding; but a crowded gallery looked on, while Benton strengthened his supporters by providing "an ample supply of cold hams, turkeys, rounds of beef, pickles, wines, and cups of hot coffee" in a near-by committee-room. Jackson gave a dinner to the "expungers" and their wives, and placed Benton at the head of the table. That the action of the Senate was unconstitutional interested no one save the lawyers, for the Bank was dead. Jackson was vindicated, and the people were enthroned.[1]

The struggle thus brought to a triumphant close was one of the severest in American political history. In 1836 the Bank obtained a charter from Pennsylvania, under the name of the Bank of the United States of Pennsylvania, and all connection between it and the Federal Government ceased. The institution and the controversies centering about it left, however, a deep impress upon the financial and political history of our fifth and sixth decades. It was the bank issue, more than anything else, that consolidated the new political parties of the period. It was that issue that

[1] MacDonald, *Jacksonian Democracy*, p. 239.

THE UNITED STATES BANK 199

proved most conclusively the hold of Jackson upon public opinion. And it was the destruction of the Bank that capped the mid-century reaction against the rampant nationalism of the decade succeeding the War of 1812. The Bank itself had been well managed, sound, and of great service to the country. But it had also showed strong monopolistic tendencies, and as a powerful capitalistic organization it ran counter to the principles and prejudices which formed the very warp and woof of Jacksonian democracy.

For more than a decade after the Bank was destroyed the United States had a troubled financial history. The payment of the last dollar of the national debt in 1834 gave point to a suggestion which Clay had repeatedly offered that, as a means of avoiding an embarrassing surplus, the proceeds of the sales of public lands should be distributed according to population among the States. One bill on this subject was killed by a veto in 1832, but another was finally approved in 1836. Before distribution could be carried far, however, the country was overtaken by the panic of 1837; and never again was there a surplus to distribute. For seven years the funds of the Government continued to be kept in state banks, until, in 1840,

THE REIGN OF ANDREW JACKSON

President Van Buren prevailed upon Congress to pass a measure setting up an independent treasury system, thereby realizing the ultimate purpose of the Jacksonians to divorce the Government from banks of every sort. When the Whigs came into power in 1841, they promptly abolished the independent Treasury with a view to resurrecting the United States Bank. Tyler's vetoes, however, frustrated their designs, and it remained for the Democrats in 1846 to revive the independent Treasury and to organize it substantially as it operates today.

CHAPTER X

THE REMOVAL OF THE SOUTHERN INDIANS

IT was not by chance that the Jacksonian period made large contribution to the working out of the ultimate relations of the red man with his white rival and conqueror. Jackson was himself an old frontier soldier, who never doubted that it was part of the natural order of things that conflict between the two peoples should go on until the weaker was dispossessed or exterminated. The era was one in which the West guided public policy; and it was the West that was chiefly interested in further circumscribing Indian lands, trade, and influence. In Jackson's day, too, the people ruled; and it was the adventurous, pushing, land-hungry common folk who decreed that the red man had lingered long enough in the Middle West and must now move on.

The pressure of the white population upon the Indian lands was felt both in the Northwest and in the Southwest; but the pressure was unevenly applied in the two sections. North of the Ohio there was simply one great glacier-like advance of the white settlers, driving westward before it practically all of the natives who did not perish in the successive attempts to roll back the wave of conquest upon the Alleghanies. The redskins were pushed from Ohio into Indiana, from Indiana into Illinois, from Illinois and Wisconsin into Iowa and Minnesota; the few tribal fragments which by treaty arrangement remained behind formed only insignificant "islands" in the midst of the fast-growing flood of white population.

In the South the great streams of migration were those that flowed down the Ohio, filling the back lands on each side, and thence down the Mississippi to its mouth. Hence, instead of pressing the natives steadily backward from a single direction, as in the North, the whites hemmed them in on east, west, and north; while to the southward the Gulf presented a relentless barrier. Powerful and populous tribes were left high and dry in Georgia, Tennessee, and Alabama — peoples who in their day of necessity could hope to find new homes only by long migrations past the settled river districts that lay upon their western frontiers.

Of these encircled tribes, four were of chief importance: the Creeks, the Cherokees, the Choctaws, and the Chickasaws. In 1825 the Creeks numbered twenty thousand, and held between five and six million acres of land in western Georgia and eastern Alabama. The Cherokees numbered about nine thousand and had even greater areas, mainly in northwestern Georgia, but to some extent also in northeastern Alabama and southeastern Tennessee. The Choctaws, numbering twenty-one thousand, and the Chickasaws, numbering thirty-six hundred, together held upwards of sixteen million acres in Mississippi — approximately the northern half of the State — and a million and a quarter acres in western Alabama. The four peoples thus numbered fifty-three thousand souls, and held ancestral lands aggregating over thirty-three million acres, or nearly the combined area of Pennsylvania and New Jersey.

Furthermore, they were no longer savages. The Creeks were the lowest in civilization; but even they had become more settled and less warlike since their chastisement by Jackson in 1814. The Choctaws and Chickasaws lived in frame houses, cultivated large stretches of land, operated workshops and mills, maintained crude but orderly

204 THE REIGN OF ANDREW JACKSON

governments, and were gradually accepting Christianity. Most advanced of all were the Cherokees. As one writer has described them, they "had horses and cattle, goats, sheep, and swine. They raised maize, cotton, tobacco, wheat, oats, and potatoes, and traded with their products to New Orleans. They had gardens, and apple and peach orchards. They had built roads, and they kept inns for travelers. They manufactured cotton and wool. . . . One of their number had invented an alphabet for their language. They had a civil government, imitated from that of the United States." Under these improved conditions, all of the tribes were growing in numbers and acquiring vested rights which it would be increasingly difficult to deny or to disregard.

A good while before Jackson entered the White House the future of these large, settled, and prosperous groups of red men began to trouble the people of Georgia, Alabama, and other Southern States. The Indians made but little use of the major part of their land; vast tracts lay untrodden save by hunters. Naturally, as the white population grew and the lands open for settlement became scarcer and poorer, the rich tribal holdings were looked upon with covetous eyes. In the

THE SOUTHERN INDIANS 205

decade following the War of 1812, when cotton cultivation was spreading rapidly over the southern interior, the demand that they be thrown open for occupation to white settlers became almost irresistible.

Three things, obviously, could happen. The tribes could be allowed to retain permanently their great domains, while the white population flowed in around them; or the lands could be opened to the whites under terms looking to a peaceful intermingling of the two peoples; or the tribes could be induced or compelled to move *en masse* to new homes beyond the Mississippi. The third plan was the only one ever considered by most people to be feasible, although it offered great difficulties and was carried out only after many delays.

The State which felt the situation most keenly was Georgia, partly because there an older and denser population pressed more eagerly for new lands, partly — it must be admitted — because lands obtained by cession were, under the practice of that State, distributed among the people by lottery. The first move in this direction was to dispossess the Creeks. As far back as 1802, when Georgia made her final cession of western lands to the United States, the latter agreed to extinguish

206 THE REIGN OF ANDREW JACKSON

the Indian title to lands within the State whenever it could be done "peaceably and on reasonable terms." This pledge the Georgians never allowed the federal authorities to forget. After 1815 several large tracts were liberated. But by that date the State wanted unbroken jurisdiction over all of the territory within her limits, and her complaints of laxness on the part of the Federal Government in bringing this about became no less frequent than vigorous.

Near the close of his Administration President Monroe sent two commissioners to procure a general cession; and at Indian Spring a treaty was concluded in which the Creeks ceded practically all of their lands between the Flint and the Chattahoochee rivers. The Senate ratified the treaty, and the Georgians were elated. But investigation showed that the Creeks who stood behind the agreement represented only an insignificant fraction of the nation, and President Adams refused to allow Troup, the irate Georgian Governor, to proceed with the intended occupation until further negotiations should have taken place. Stormy exchanges of views followed, in the course of which the Governor more than once reminded Adams that Georgia was "sovereign on her own soil." But in

THE SOUTHERN INDIANS 207

1826 and 1827 treaties were obtained finally extinguishing Creek titles in the State. Land west of the Mississippi was promised to all Creeks who would go there.

The problem of the Cherokees was more difficult. By a series of treaties beginning in 1785 the United States had recognized this people as a nation, capable of making peace and war, of owning the lands within its boundaries, and of governing and punishing its own citizens by its own laws. At the close of Jefferson's second Administration the tribe seriously considered moving west of the Mississippi, and shortly after the War of 1812 most of the northern members resident in Tennessee took the long-deferred step. The refusal of the Georgia members to go with the Tennesseeans disappointed the land-hungry whites, and from that time the authorities of the State labored incessantly both to break down the notion that the Cherokees were a "nation" to be dealt with through diplomatic channels, and to extend over them, in effect, the full sovereignty of the State. In December, 1828, the Legislature took the bold step of enacting that all white persons in the Cherokee territory should be subject to the laws of Georgia; that after June 1, 1830, all Indians resident in this territory should

208 THE REIGN OF ANDREW JACKSON

be subject to such laws as might be prescribed for them by the State; and that after this date all laws made by the Cherokee Government should be null and void.

When Jackson became President he found on his desk a vigorous protest against this drastic piece of legislation. But appeal to him was useless. He was on record as believing, in common with most southwesterners, that Georgia had a rightful jurisdiction over her Indian lands; and his Secretary of War, Eaton, was instructed to say to the Cherokee representatives that their people would be expected either to yield to Georgia's authority or to remove beyond the Mississippi. In his first annual message, on December 8, 1829, the President set forth the principles that guided him from first to last in dealing with the Indian problem. It would be greatly to the interest of the Indians themselves, he said, to remove to the ample lands that would be set apart for them permanently in the West, where each tribe could have its own home and its own government, subject to no control by the United States except for the maintenance of peace on the frontier and among the tribes. Forcible removal was not to be contemplated; that would be cruel and unjust. But every effort was to be made to bring about a voluntary migration. One thing was to be clearly understood: any tribe or group that chose to remain in Georgia must submit to the laws of the State and yield its claim to all land which had not been improved. The President was not indifferent to the well-being of the red men; but he refused to recognize the Cherokees as a "nation" having "rights" as against either Georgia or the United States. A few weeks after the message was received Congress passed a bill creating an Indian reservation beyond the Mississippi and appropriating five hundred thousand dollars to aid in the removal of such Indians as should choose to accept the offer of the Government.

The outlook for the Cherokees was now dark. Both the executive and legislative branches of the Federal Government were committed to a policy which offered only the alternatives of removal or subjection; and, thus encouraged, the Georgia Legislature voted to proceed with the extension of the full authority of the State over both the Cherokees and the Creeks after June 1, 1830. To make matters worse, the discovery of gold in the northeastern corner of the State in 1829 brought down upon the Cherokee lands a horde of scrambling, lawless fortune seekers, numbered already in 1830 by the thousand. None the less, the Cherokee opposition stiffened. The Indian legislative council voted that all who accepted lands beyond the Mississippi and settled on them should forfeit their tribal membership, that those who sold their individual property to emigrate should be flogged, and that those who voted to sell a part or all of the tribal possessions should be put to death.

One resource remained to be exhausted in defense of the Indian claims; this was the courts. But here again things went unfavorably. After many delays a test case, Cherokee Nation *vs.* State of Georgia, was placed upon the docket of the Supreme Court. The bill set forth the plaintiff to be "the Cherokee Nation of Indians, a foreign State, not owning allegiance to the United States, nor to any State of this union, nor to any prince, potentate, or State other than their own," and it asked that the Court declare null the Georgia Acts of 1828 and 1829 and enjoin the Georgia officials from interfering with Cherokee lands, mines, and other property, or with the persons of Cherokees on account of anything done by them within the Cherokee territory. The Indians were represented before the Court by two attorneys, one of them being William Wirt; Georgia employed no counsel. The

THE SOUTHERN INDIANS 211

opinion of the Court as announced at the January term, 1831, by Chief Justice Marshall was that while the Cherokee nation was a State and had uniformly been dealt with as such by the Federal Government since 1789, it was not a "foreign State" within the meaning of the Constitution, and therefore was not entitled to sue in that character in the courts of the United States. "If it be true," the decision concluded, "that wrongs have been inflicted and that still greater are to be apprehended, this is not the tribunal which can redress the past or prevent the future. The motion for an injunction is denied."

The case was thus thrown out of court. Yet the Cherokees were recognized as a "domestic, dependent" nation, and there was nothing in the decision to indicate that the extension of the laws of Georgia over them was valid and constitutional. Indeed, in a second case that came up shortly, Worcester *vs*. State of Georgia, the Court strongly backed up the Indians' contention. Worcester was a Presbyterian missionary who was imprisoned for violation of a Georgia statute forbidding white persons to reside in the Cherokee territory without a license. The case was appealed to the Supreme Court, and in the decision of March 10, 1832,

Marshall affirmed the status of the Cherokees as a "nation" within whose territory "the laws of Georgia can have no force, and which the citizens of Georgia have no right to enter but with the assent of the Cherokees themselves or in conformity with treaties and with the acts of Congress." The statute was accordingly declared to be unconstitutional and Worcester was ordered to be discharged.

This ought to have been enough to protect the Cherokees in their rights. But it was not, and for two reasons: the contempt of Georgia for the Court's opinions, and the refusal of Jackson to restrain the State in its headstrong course. Already the state authorities had refused to take notice of a writ of error to the Supreme Court sued out in December, 1830, in behalf of a condemned Cherokee, Corn Tassel, and had permitted the execution of the unfortunate redskin. The state court now refused to issue a writ of *habeas corpus* in behalf of Worcester, and the prisoner was held — precisely as if the law under which he was convicted had been pronounced constitutional — until he was pardoned by the Governor a year later.

This action on the part of the State was, of

THE SOUTHERN INDIANS 213

course, nothing less than nullification. Yet Jackson did not lift a finger. "John Marshall has made his decision," he is reported to have said; "now let him enforce it." The South Carolinians were quick to seize upon the inconsistencies of the situation. Nullification in their State was apparently one thing; in Georgia, quite another. The very fact, however, that the Georgians had successfully defied the federal Supreme Court did much to encourage their neighbors in a course of similar boldness. Jackson's leniency toward Georgia has never been wholly explained. He was undoubtedly influenced by his sympathy with the purpose of the State to establish its jurisdiction over all lands within its borders. Furthermore he cherished an antipathy for Marshall which even led him to refuse in 1835 to attend a memorial meeting in the great jurist's honor. But these considerations do not wholly cover the case. All that the historian can say is that the President chose to take notice of the threats and acts of South Carolina and to ignore the threats and acts of Georgia, without ever being troubled by the inconsistency of his course. His political career affords many such illustrations of the arbitrary and even erratic character of his mind.

Meanwhile the great Indian migration was setting in. Emulating the example of Georgia, Alabama and Mississippi extended their laws over all of the Indian lands within their boundaries; and in all parts of the South the red folk — some of them joyously, but most of them sorrowfully — prepared to take up their long journey. In 1832 the Creeks yielded to the United States all of their remaining lands east of the Mississippi. By the spring of 1833 the Choctaws and Chickasaws had done the same thing and were on their way westward. Only the Cherokees remained, and in his message of December 3, 1833, Jackson reiterated his earlier arguments for their removal. Realizing that further resistance was useless, a portion of the tribe signified its readiness to go. The remainder, however, held out, and it was only at the close of 1835 that the long-desired treaty of cession could be secured. All Cherokee lands east of the Mississippi were now relinquished to the United States, which agreed to pay five million dollars for them, to provide an adequate home in the new Indian Territory created by Congress during the preceding year, and to bear all the costs of removing the tribe thither.

It was not alone the South, however, that

THE SOUTHERN INDIANS 215

witnessed widespread displacements of Indian populations in the Jacksonian period. How the Black Hawk War of 1832 grew out of, and in turn led to, removals in the remoter Northwest has been related in another volume in this series.[1] And, in almost every western State, surviving Indian titles were rapidly extinguished. Between 1829 and 1837 ninety-four Indian treaties, most of them providing for transfers of territory, were concluded; and before Jackson went out of office he was able to report to Congress that, "with the exception of two small bands living in Ohio and Indiana, not exceeding fifteen hundred persons, and of the Cherokees, all of the tribes on the east side of the Mississippi, and extending from Lake Michigan to Florida, have entered into engagements which will lead to their transplantation." With little delay the Cherokees, too, were added to this list, although a group of irreconcilables resisted until 1838, when they were forcibly ejected by a contingent of United States troops under General Winfield Scott.

All of this was done not without strong protest from other people besides the Indians. Some who

[1] See *The Old Northwest*, by Frederic Austin Ogg (in *The Chronicles of America*).

objected did so for political effect. When Clay and Calhoun, for example, thundered in the Senate against the removal treaties, they were merely seeking to discredit the Administration; both held views on Indian policy which were substantially the same as Jackson's. But there was also objection on humanitarian grounds; and the Society of Friends and other religious bodies engaged in converting and educating the southern tribes used all possible influence to defeat the plan of removal. On the whole, however, the country approved what was being done. People felt that the further presence of large, organized bodies of natives in the midst of a rapidly growing white population, and of tribes setting themselves up as quasi-independent nations within the bounds of the States, was an anomaly that could not last; and they considered that, distressing as were many features of the removals, both white man and red man would ultimately be better off.

CHAPTER XI

THE JACKSONIAN SUCCESSION

"OH, hang General Jackson," exclaimed Fanny Kemble one day, after dinner, in the cabin of the ship that brought her, in the summer of 1832, to the United States. Even before she set foot on our shores, the brilliant English actress was tired of the din of politics and bored by the incessant repetition of the President's name. Subsequently she was presented at the White House and had an opportunity to form her own opinion of the "monarch" whose name and deeds were on everybody's lips; and the impression was by no means unfavorable. "Very tall and thin he was," says her journal, "but erect and dignified; a good specimen of a fine old, well-battered soldier; his manners perfectly simple and quiet, and, therefore, very good."

Small wonder that the name of Jackson was heard wherever men and women congregated in

218 THE REIGN OF ANDREW JACKSON

1832! Something more than half of the people of the country were at the moment trying to elect the General to a second term as President, and something less than half were putting forth their best efforts to prevent such a "calamity." Three years of Jacksonian rule had seen the civil service revolutionized, the Cabinet banished from its traditional place in the governmental system, and the conduct of the executive branch given a wholly new character and bent. Internal improvements had been checked by the Maysville Road veto. The United States Bank had been given a blow, through another veto, which sent it staggering. Political fortunes had been made and unmade by a wave of the President's hand. The first attempt of a State to put the stability of the Union to the test had brought the Chief Executive dramatically into the rôle of defender of the nation's dignity and perpetuity. No previous President had so frequently challenged the attention of the public; none had kept himself more continuously in the forefront of political controversy.

Frail health and close application to official duties prevented Jackson from traveling extensively during his eight years in the White House. He saw the Hermitage but once in this time, and

THE JACKSONIAN SUCCESSION 219

on but one occasion did he venture far from the capital. This was in the summer of 1833, when he toured the Middle States and New England northward as far as Concord, New Hampshire. Accompanied by Van Buren, Lewis Cass, Levi Woodbury, and other men of prominence, the President set off from Washington in early June. At Baltimore, Philadelphia, New York, and intervening cities the party was received with all possible demonstrations of regard. Processions moved through crowded streets; artillery thundered salutes; banquet followed banquet; the enthusiasm of the masses was unrestrained. At New York the furnishings of the hotel suite occupied by the President were eventually auctioned off as mementoes of the occasion.

New England was, in the main, enemy country. None the less, the President was received there with unstinted goodwill. Edward Everett said that only two other men had ever been welcomed in Boston as Jackson was. They were Washington and La Fayette. The President's determined stand against nullification was fresh in mind, and the people, regardless of party, were not slow to express their appreciation. Their cordiality was fully reciprocated. "He is amazingly tickled with the Yankees," reports a fellow traveler more noted for veracity than for elegance of speech, "and the more he sees on 'em, the better he likes 'em. 'No nullification here,' says he. 'No,' says I, 'General; Mr. Calhoun would stand no more chance down east than a stumped-tail bull in fly time.'"

To the infinite disgust of John Quincy Adams, Harvard University conferred upon the distinguished visitor the honorary degree of doctor of laws. In the course of the ceremony one of the seniors delivered, in Latin, a salutatory concluding with the words: "Harvard welcomes Jackson the President. She embraces Jackson the Patriot." "A splendid compliment, sir, a splendid compliment," declared the honored guest after Woodbury had translated the phrases for his benefit; "but why talk about so live a thing as patriotism in a dead language?" At the close of the exercises the students filed past the President and were introduced to him, each greeting him, "to the infinite edification and amusement of the grizzly old warrior," by his new title *Doctor* Jackson. The wits of the opposition lost no opportunity to poke fun at the President's accession to the brotherhood of scholars. As he was closing a speech some days

THE JACKSONIAN SUCCESSION 221

later an auditor called out, "You must give them a little Latin, *Doctor*." In nowise abashed, the President solemnly doffed his hat again, stepped to the front of the platform, and resumed: "*E pluribus unum*, my friends, *sine qua non!*"

Life at the White House, as one writer has remarked, lost under Jackson something of the good form of the Virginia régime, but it lost nothing of the air of domesticity. Throughout the two Administrations the mistress of the mansion was Mrs. Andrew Jackson Donelson, wife of the President's secretary and in every respect a very capable woman. Of formality there was little or none. Major Lewis was a member of the presidential household, and other intimates — Van Buren, Kendall, Blair, Hill — dropped in at any time, "before breakfast, or in the evening, as inclination prompted." The President was always accessible to callers, whether or not their business was important. Yet he found much time, especially in the evenings, for the enjoyment of his long reed pipe with red clay bowl, in the intimacy of the White House living room, with perhaps a Cabinet officer to read dispatches or other state papers to him in a corner, while the ladies sewed and chatted and half a dozen children played about the room.

Social affairs there were, of course. But they were simple enough to please the most ardent Jeffersonian — much too simple to please people accustomed to somewhat rigorous etiquette. Thus George Bancroft, who had the reputation of being one of Washington's most punctilious gentlemen, thought well of Jackson's character but very poorly of his levees. In describing a White House reception which he attended in 1831, he wrote:

The old man stood in the center of a little circle, about large enough for a cotillion, and shook hands with everybody that offered. The number of ladies who attended was small; nor were they brilliant. But to compensate for it there was a throng of apprentices, boys of all ages, men not civilized enough to walk about the room with their hats off; the vilest promiscuous medley that ever was congregated in a decent house; many of the lowest gathering round the doors, pouncing with avidity upon the wine and refreshments, tearing the cake with the ravenous keenness of intense hunger; starvelings, and fellows with dirty faces and dirty manners; all the refuse that Washington could turn forth from its workshops and stables.

The "people" still ruled. Yet it was only the public receptions that presented such scenes of disorder. The dinners which the President occasionally gave were well appointed. A Philadelphia

THE JACKSONIAN SUCCESSION 223

gentleman who was once invited to the White House with two or three friends testifies that "the dinner was very neat and served in excellent taste, while the wines were of the choicest qualities. The President himself dined on the simplest fare: bread, milk, and vegetables."

Jackson was never a rich man, and throughout his stay in the White House he found it no easy matter to make ends meet. He entertained his personal friends and official guests royally. He lavished hospitality upon the general public, sometimes spending as much as a thousand or fifteen hundred dollars on a single levee. He drew a sharp line between personal and public expenditures, and met out of his own pocket outlays that under administrations both before and after were charged to the public account. He loaned many thousands of dollars, in small amounts, to needy friends, to old comrades in arms, and especially to widows and orphans of his soldiery and of his political supporters; and a large proportion of these debts he not only never collected but actually forgot. Receipts from the Hermitage farm during his years of absence were small, and fire in 1834 made necessary a rebuilding of the family residence at considerable cost. The upshot was that when, in 1837, the

224 THE REIGN OF ANDREW JACKSON

General was preparing to leave Washington, he had to scrape together every available dollar in cash, and in addition pledge the cotton crop of his plantation six months ahead for a loan of six thousand dollars, in order to pay the bills outstanding against him in the capital.

Meanwhile the country came to the election of 1836. From the time of Van Buren's withdrawal from the Cabinet in 1831 to become, with Jackson's full approval, a candidate for the vice presidency, there never was doubt that the New Yorker would be the Democratic presidential nominee in 1836, or that his election would mean a continuation, in most respects, of the Jacksonian régime. Never did a President more clearly pick his successor. There was, of course, some protest within the party. Van Buren was not popular, and it required all of the personal and official influence that the President could bring to bear, backed up by judicious use of the patronage, to carry his program through. At that, his own State rebelled and, through a resolution of the Legislature, put itself behind the candidacy of Senator Hugh L. White. The bold actions of his second Administration, defiant alike of precedent and opposition, had alienated many of the President's more intelligent and

THE JACKSONIAN SUCCESSION 225

conservative followers. Yet the allegiance of the masses was unshaken; and when the Democratic convention assembled at Baltimore in May, 1835, — a year and a half before the election — the nomination of Van Buren was secured without a dissenting vote. There was no need to adopt a platform; everybody understood that Jackson's policies were the platform, and that Jackson himself was as truly before the electorate as if he had been a candidate for a third term. In his letter of acceptance Van Buren met all expectations by declaring his purpose "to tread generally in the footsteps of President Jackson."

The anti-Administration forces entered the campaign with no flattering prospects. Since 1832 their opposition to "executive usurpation" had won for them a new party name, "Whig." But neither their opposition nor any other circumstance had given them party solidarity. National Republicans, anti-Masons, converted Jacksonians, state rights men — upon what broad and constructive platform could they hope to unite? They had no lack of able presidential aspirants. There was Clay, the National Republican candidate in 1832; there was Webster, of whom Jackson once said that he would never be President because he was "too far east, knows too much, and is too honest"; and there were lesser lights, such as Judge John McLean. But, again, how could the many discordant groups be rallied to the support of any single leader?

Jackson predicted in 1834 that his opponents would nominate William Henry Harrison, because "they have got to take up a soldier; they have tried orators enough." The prophecy was a shrewd one, and in 1840 it was fulfilled to the letter. Upon the present occasion, however, the leaders decided to place no single nominee in the field, but rather to bring forward a number of candidates who could be expected to develop local strength and so to split the vote as to throw the final choice into the House of Representatives. This seemed the only hope of circumventing Van Buren's election. Four sectional candidates entered the race: Webster was backed by New England; the Northwest united on Harrison; the Southwest joined the Tennessee revolters in support of White; Ohio had her own candidate in the person of McLean.

The plan was ingenious, but it did not work. Van Buren received 170 electoral votes against 124 in spite of his opponents. He carried fifteen of the twenty-six States, including four in New England.

THE JACKSONIAN SUCCESSION 227

Harrison received 73 votes, White 26 (including those of Tennessee), and Webster 14. South Carolina refused to support any of the candidates on either side and threw away her votes on W. P. Mangum of North Carolina. The Democrats kept control of both branches of Congress.

Victory, therefore, rested with the Jacksonians — which means with Jackson himself. The Democrats would have control of both the executive and legislative branches of the Government for some years to come; the Bank would not soon be rechartered; the veto power would remain intact; federal expenditure upon internal improvements had been curbed, and the "American system" had been checked; the national debt was discharged and revenue was superabundant; Jackson could look back over the record of his Administrations with pride and forward to the rule of "Little Van" with satisfaction. "When I review the arduous administration through which I have passed," declared the President soon after the results of the election were made known, "the formidable opposition, to its very close, of the combined talents, wealth, and power of the whole aristocracy of the United States, aided as it is by the moneyed monopolies of the whole country with their corrupting influence, with which we had to contend, I am truly thankful to my God for this happy result."

Congress met on the 5th of December for the closing session of the Administration. The note of victory pervaded the President's message. Yet there was one more triumph to be won: the resolution of censure voted by the Senate in 1834 was still officially on the record book. Now it was that Benton finally procured the passage of his expunging resolution, although not until both branches of Congress had been dragged into controversy more personal and acrid, if possible, than any in the past eight years. The action taken was probably unconstitutional. But Jackson's "honor" was vindicated, and that was all that he and his friends saw, or cared to see, in the proceeding.

As early as 1831 the President conceived the idea of issuing a farewell address to the people upon the eve of his retirement; and a few weeks before the election of Van Buren he sent to Taney a list of subjects which he proposed to touch upon in the document, requesting him to "throw on paper" his ideas concerning them. The address was issued on March 4, 1837, and followed closely the copy subsequently found in Taney's handwriting in the Jackson manuscripts. Its contents were thoroughly commonplace, being indeed hardly more than a résumé of the eight annual messages; and it might well have been dismissed as the amiable musings of a garrulous old man. But nothing associated with the name of Jackson ever failed to stir controversy. The Whigs ridiculed the egotism which underlay the palpable imitation of Washington. "Happily," said the New York *American*, "it is the last humbug which the mischievous popularity of this illiterate, violent, vain, and iron-willed soldier can impose upon a confiding and credulous people." The Democrats, however, lauded the address, praised the wisdom and sincerity of its author, and laid away among their most valued mementoes the white satin copies which admiring friends scattered broadcast over the country.

Showered with evidences of undiminished popularity, the General came down to his last day in office. One enthusiast sent him a light wagon made entirely of hickory sticks with the bark upon them. Another presented a phaeton made of wood taken from the old frigate *Constitution*. A third capped the climax by forwarding from New York a cheese four feet in diameter, two feet thick, and weighing fourteen hundred pounds — twice as large, the *Globe* fondly pointed out, as the cheese presented to Jefferson under similar circumstances a quarter of a century earlier. From all parts of the country came callers, singly and in delegations, to pay their respects and to assure the outgoing Chief of their goodwill and admiration. March 4, 1837, was a raw, disagreeable day. But Jackson, pale and racked by disease, rode with his chosen successor to the place where he had himself assumed office eight years before, and sat uncovered while the oath was administered and the inaugural delivered. The suave, elegantly dressed Van Buren was politely applauded as the new Chief to whom respect was due. But it was the tall, haggard, white-haired soldier-politician who had put Van Buren where he was who awoke the spontaneous enthusiasm of the crowds.

Three days after the inauguration Jackson started for the Hermitage. His trip became a series of ovations, and he was obliged several times to pause for rest. At last he reached Nashville, where once again, as in the old days of the Indian wars, he was received with an acclaim deeply tinged by personal friendship and neighborly pride. A great banquet in his honor was presided over by James K. Polk, now Speaker of the national House

THE JACKSONIAN SUCCESSION 231

of Representatives; and the orators vied one with another in extolling his virtues and depicting his services to the country. Then Jackson went on to the homestead whose seclusion he coveted.

No one knew better than the ex-President himself that his course was almost run. He was seventy years of age and seldom free from pain for an hour. He considered himself, moreover, a poor man — mainly, it appears, because he went back to Tennessee owing ten thousand dollars and with only ninety dollars in his pockets. He was, however, only "land poor," for his plantation of twenty-six hundred acres was rich and valuable, and he had a hundred and forty slaves — "servants" he always called them — besides large numbers of horses and cattle. A year or two of thrifty supervision brought his lands and herds back to liberal yields; his debts were soon paid off; and notwithstanding heavy outlays for his adopted son, whose investments invariably turned out badly, he was soon able to put aside all anxiety over pecuniary matters.

Established again in his old home, surrounded by congenial relatives and friends, respected by neighbors without regard to politics, and visited from time to time by notable foreigners and Americans,

Jackson found much of satisfaction in his declining years. For a time he fully lived up to the promise made to Benton and Blair that he would keep clear of politics. His interest in the fortunes of his party, however, was not diminished by his retirement from public life. He corresponded freely with Van Buren, whose policies he in most respects approved; and as the campaign of 1840 approached the "old war-horse began once more to sniff the battle from afar." Admitting to his friends that the situation looked "a little dubious," he exerted himself powerfully to bring about the reëlection of the New Yorker. He wrote a letter belittling the military qualities of the Whig candidate, thereby probably doing the Democratic cause more harm than good; and finally, to avert the humiliation of a Whig victory in Tennessee, he "took the stump" and denounced the enemy up and down through all western Tennessee and southern Kentucky. But "Tippecanoe and Tyler too" was too much for him; the Whig candidates carried both Tennessee and Kentucky and won the nation-wide contest by 234 to 60 electoral votes.

The old warrior took the defeat — *his* defeat, he always regarded it — philosophically, and at once began to lay plans for a recovery of Democratic

THE JACKSONIAN SUCCESSION 233

supremacy in 1844. For another quadrennium his hand was on the party throttle. When men speculated as to whether Van Buren, General Cass, General Butler, or Senator Benton would be the standard bearer in 1844, they always asked what Jackson's edict on the subject would be; and the final selection of James K. Polk, while not fully dictated by the ex-President, was the result of a compromise in which his advice played a prominent part. Though past seventy-seven and hardly able to sign his name, Jackson threw himself into the campaign and undoubtedly contributed to the election of his fellow-Tennesseean. His satisfaction with the outcome and with the annexation of Texas which quickly followed found expression in a barbecue attended by all the Democrats of the neighborhood and by some of note from a distance. "We have restored the Government to sound principles," declared the host in a brief, faltering speech from the Hermitage portico, "and extended the area of our institutions to the Rio Grande. Now for Oregon and Fifty-four-forty."

Oregon — although not to fifty-four forty — was soon to be duly made American soil. But Jackson did not live to witness the event. Early in 1845 his health began to fail rapidly and on the

234 THE REIGN OF ANDREW JACKSON

very day of Polk's inauguration he was at the point of death. Rallying, he struggled manfully for three months against the combined effects of consumption, dropsy, and dysentery. But on Sunday, the 8th of June, the end came. In accordance with a pledge which he had given his wife years before, he had become a communicant of the Presbyterian church; and his last words to the friends about his bedside were messages of Christian cheer. After two days the body was laid to rest in the Hermitage garden, beside the grave of the companion whose loss he had never ceased to mourn with all the feeling of which his great nature was capable. The authorities at the national capital ordered public honors to be paid to the ex-President, and gatherings in all parts of the country listened with much show of feeling to appropriate eulogies.

"General Jackson," said Daniel Webster to Thurlow Weed in 1837, "is an honest and upright man. He does what he thinks is right, and does it with all his might. He has a violent temper, which leads him often to hasty conclusions. It also causes him to view as personal to himself the public acts of other men. For this reason there is great difference between Jackson angry and Jackson in

THE JACKSONIAN SUCCESSION 235

good humor. When he is calm, his judgment is good; when angry, it is usually bad. . . . His patriotism is no more to be questioned than that of Washington. He is the greatest General we have and, except Washington, the greatest we ever had."

To this characterization of Andrew Jackson by his greatest American contemporary it is impossible to make noteworthy addition. His was a character of striking contradictions. His personal virtues were honesty, bravery, open-heartedness, chivalry toward women, hospitality, steadfastness. His personal faults were irascibility, egotism, stubbornness, vindictiveness, and intolerance of the opinions of others. He was not a statesman; yet some of the highest qualities of statesmanship were in him. He had a perception of the public will which has rarely been surpassed; and in most, if not all, of the great issues of his time he had a grasp of the right end of the question.

The country came to the belief that the National Bank should not be revived. It accepted and perpetuated Van Buren's independent treasury plan. The annexation of Texas, which Jackson strongly favored, became an accomplished fact with the approval of a majority of the people. The moderated protective tariff to which Jackson inclined was kept up until the Civil War. The removal of the Indians to reservations beyond the Mississippi fell in with the views of the public upon that subject and inaugurated an Indian policy which was closely adhered to for more than half a century. In his vindication of executive independence Jackson broke new ground, crudely enough it is true; yet, whatever the merits of his ideas at the moment, they reshaped men's conception of the presidency and helped make that office the power that it is today. The strong stand taken against nullification clarified popular opinion upon the nature of the Union and lent new and powerful support to national vigor and dignity.

Over against these achievements must be placed the introduction of the Spoils System, which debauched the Civil Service and did the country lasting harm; yet Jackson only responded to public opinion which held "rotation in office to be the cardinal principle of democracy." It needed a half-century of experience to convince the American people of this fallacy and to place the national Civil Service beyond the reach of spoilsmen. Even now public opinion is slow to realize that efficiency in office can be secured only by experience and relative permanence.

BIBLIOGRAPHICAL NOTE

THE events of the period covered in this volume are described with some fullness in all of the general American histories. Of these, two are especially noteworthy for literary quality and other elements of popular interest: Woodrow Wilson's *History of the American People*, 5 vols. (1902), and John B. McMaster's *History of the People of the United States*, 8 vols. (1883–1913). The Jacksonian epoch is treated in Wilson's fourth volume and in McMaster's fifth and sixth volumes. On similar lines, but with more emphasis on political and constitutional matters, is James Schouler's *History of the United States under the Constitution*, 7 vols. (1880–1913), vols. III–IV. One seeking a scholarly view of the period, in an adequate literary setting, can hardly do better, however, than to read Frederick J. Turner's *Rise of the New West* (1906) and William MacDonald's *Jacksonian Democracy* (1906). These are volumes XIV and XV in *The American Nation*, edited by Albert B. Hart.

Biographies are numerous and in a number of instances excellent. Of lives of Jackson, upwards of a dozen have been published. The most recent and in every respect the best is John S. Bassett's *Life of Andrew Jackson*, 2 vols. (1911). This work is based throughout on the sources; its literary quality is above the average;

and it appraises Jackson and his times in an unimpeachable spirit of fairness. Within very limited space, William G. Brown's *Andrew Jackson* (1900) tells the story of Jackson admirably; and a good biography, marred only by a lack of sympathy and by occasional inaccuracy in details, is William G. Sumner's *Andrew Jackson* (rev. ed., 1899). Of older biographies, the most important is James Parton's *Life of Andrew Jackson*, 3 vols. (1861). This work is sketchy, full of irrelevant or unimportant matter, and uncritical; but for a half-century it was the repository from which historians and biographers chiefly drew in dealing with Jackson's epoch. John H. Eaton's *Life of Andrew Jackson* (1842) describes Jackson's earlier career, mainly on the military side; but it never rises above the level of a campaign document.

Among biographies of Jackson's contemporaries may be mentioned George T. Curtis, *Life of Daniel Webster*, 2 vols. (1870); Henry C. Lodge, *Daniel Webster* (1883); John B. McMaster, *Daniel Webster* (1902); Frederic A. Ogg, *Daniel Webster* (1914); Carl Schurz, *Henry Clay*, 2 vols. (1887); Gaillard Hunt, *John C. Calhoun* (1908); William M. Meigs, *The Life of John Caldwell Calhoun*, 2 vols. (1917); John T. Morse, *John Quincy Adams* (1882); Edward M. Shepard, *Martin Van Buren* (1888); Theodore Roosevelt, *Thomas Hart Benton* (1888); and Theodore D. Jervey, *Robert Y. Hayne and His Times* (1909).

On many topics the reader will do well to go to monographs or other special works. Thus Jackson's policy of removals from public office is presented with good perspective in Carl R. Fish, *The Civil Service and the Patronage* (Harvard Historical Studies, XI, 1905). The history of the bank controversy is best told in Ralph C. H. Catterall, *The Second Bank of the United States* (1903); and interesting chapters in the country's financial history are presented in Edward G. Bourne, *History of the Surplus Revenue of 1837* (1885), and David Kinley, *The History, Organization, and Influence of the Independent Treasury of the United States* (1893). On the tariff one should consult Frank W. Taussig, *Tariff History of the United States* (6th ed., 1914) and Edward Stanwood, *American Tariff Controversies*, 2 vols. (1903). Similarly illuminating studies of nullification are David F. Houston, *Critical Study of Nullification in South Carolina* (Harvard Historical Studies, III, 1896) and Ulrich B. Phillips, *Georgia and State Rights* (American Historical Association Reports, 1901, II).

Aside from newspapers, and from collections of public documents of private correspondence, which cannot be enumerated here, the source materials for the period fall into two main classes: books of autobiography and reminiscence, and the writings of travelers. Most conspicuous in the first group is Thomas H. Benton, *Thirty Years' View; or, a History of the Working of the American Government for Thirty Years, from 1820 to 1850*, 2 vols. (1854). Benton was an active member of the Senate throughout the Jacksonian period, and his book gives an interesting and valuable first-hand account of the public affairs of the time. Amos Kendall's *Autobiography* (1872) is, unfortunately, hardly more than a collection of papers and scattered memoranda. Nathan Sargent's *Public Men and Events, 1817–1853*, 2 vols. (1875), consists of chatty sketches, with an anti-Jackson slant. Other books of contemporary reminiscence are Lyman Beecher's *Autobiography*, 2 vols. (1863–65);

Robert Mayo's *Political Sketches of Eight Years in Washington* (1839); and S. C. Goodrich's *Recollections of a Lifetime*, 2 vols. (1856). The one monumental diary is John Quincy Adams, *Memoirs; Comprising Portions of his Diary from 1795 to 1848* (ed. by Charles F. Adams, 12 vols., 1874–77). All things considered, there is no more important nonofficial source for the period.

In Jackson's day the United States was visited by an extraordinary number of Europeans who forthwith wrote books descriptive of what they had seen. Two of the most interesting — although the least flattering — of these works are Charles Dickens's *American Notes for General Circulation* (1842, and many reprints) and Mrs. Frances E. Trollope's *Domestic Manners of the Americans* (1832). Two very readable and generally sympathetic English accounts are Frances A. Kemble's *Journal, 1832–1833*, 2 vols. (1835) and Harriet Martineau's *Society in America*, 3 vols. (2d ed., 1837). The principal French work of the sort is M. Chevalier, *Society, Manners, and Politics in the United States* (Eng. trans. from 3d French ed., 1839). Political conditions in the country are described in Alexis de Tocqueville, *Democracy in America* (Eng. trans. by Reeve in 2 vols., 1862), and the economic situation is set forth in detail in James S. Buckingham, *America, Historical, Statistical and Descriptive*, 2 vols. (1841), and *The Slave States of America*, 2 vols. (1842).

INDEX

Adams, John, Jackson makes acquaintance of, 17

Adams, J. Q., Secretary of State, and Jackson's Florida expedition, 62, 63, 64; candidate for presidency, 76–77, 82–83, 84, 86, 87, 88–93; and Jackson, 80, 93–94, 108, 122, 220; diary quoted, 88, 109; "corrupt bargain," 89–92, 96; elected, 93; as President, 95–100, 104–106; personal characteristics, 96–97; abolishes patronage, 97–98; and internal improvements, 99, 100, 105; candidate for reëlection (1828), 106, 109–110; no enthusiasm for, 113; on Calhoun, 139; and Indian question, 206; biography, 238

Alabama, Indians in, 202, 203, 204, 214

Ambrister, Robert, 58

American, New York, quoted, 229

Apalachicola River, Nicholls builds fort on, 53; Jackson's army marches down, 57

Arbuthnot, Alexander, 53, 58

Aurora, Pennsylvania newspaper, 193

Baltimore, welcomes Jackson, 64, 219; Democratic convention at (1835), 225

Bancroft, George, quoted, 222

Bank, United States, Jackson's attitude toward, 79, 184–88; Adams and, 99; established, 138, 182; and the South, 140; war on, 181–200; Congress supports, 187; Jackson plans reorganization of, 187; bill to recharter, 189–91; bill vetoed, 190, 218; as political issue, 191; believed insolvent by Jackson, 192–93; removal of deposits, 193–95; senate censures Jackson for removal, 196–98; Whigs try to resurrect (1841), 200; bibliography, 239

Barry, W. T., Postmaster-General, 118

Bassett, J. S., biographer of Jackson, cited, 4, 238; quoted, 37

Benton, Jesse, Jackson encounters, 21, 33

Benton, T. H., 26, 149, 232, 233; Jackson fights with, 21, 33; quoted, 49, 113, 167; introduces bills against Adams, 105; on Van Buren's defeat as minister, 136; on Foote's resolution, 144; on Hayne, 147; and United States Bank question, 190–91, 195; and censure of Jackson, 197; biography, 238

Berrien, J. M., Attorney-General, 118

Biddle, Nicholas, President of United States Bank, 183, 184, 185–86, 187, 188, 189, 192, 195

Black Hawk War, 215

Blair, F. P., editor of the *Globe*, 130, 193, 221, 232

Blount, William, 17; Governor of Tennessee, 26, 28, 30, 35, 55, 74

INDEX

Borgne, Lake, British army at, 40

Boston, endorses Jackson's proclamation to South Carolina, 176; welcomes President Jackson, 219

Bowyer, Fort, British attempt to destroy, 39

Branch, John, Secretary of Navy, 118

Brown, Jacob, of New York, 51

Buchanan, James, author of "corrupt bargain," 90

Burr, Aaron, Jackson makes acquaintance of, 17; opinion of Jackson, 73

Butler, General, 233

Cabinet, Jackson's, 117–18, 129–130, 135–36, 193–94, 218; Kitchen, 130–31

Cadwalader, General Thomas, 110, 184

Calhoun, J. C., father makes home at Waxhaw, 5; Secretary of War, and Jackson's Florida expedition, 56, 62, 135; aspirant for presidency, 77–78, 87, 103, 131; Jackson's attitude toward, 80; candidate for vice presidency, 84; elected, 85; described by Adams, 109; reelected to vice presidency, 110; Eaton controversy, 132–134; against Van Buren, 134; sectionalist, 139; at Hayne-Webster debate, 149; change in political ideas, 159; *Exposition*, 161, 168; and nullification, 161, 162, 164–65, 166, 167–68, 171, 172; seeks support of South Carolina, 162; *Address to the People of South Carolina*, 168; *Fort Hill Letter*, 168; and tariff, 169; resigns vice presidency, 172; in Senate, 172, 196; on Indian policy, 216; bibliography, 238

Calhoun, Mrs. J. C., 134

Calhoun, Rebecca, marries Andrew Pickens, 5

Callava, José, Governor of Florida, 58–59, 65, 66, 67

Campbell, G. W., Senator from Tennessee, 23

Carrickfergus (Ireland), home of Jackson's father, 1, 9

Carroll, William, 111

Cass, Lewis, Secretary of War, 136; accompanies Jackson to New England, 219; possible candidate for presidency, 233

Castlereagh, Robert Stewart, Lord Viscount, quoted, 61

Caucus as nominating device, 81–82, 84

Charleston (S. C.), Andrew Jackson's father arrives at, 1; Jackson in, 9–10; preparations against, 173; nullifiers meet at, 178

Cherokee Indians, number, 203; location, 203; civilization, 204; and Georgia, 207–13; treaty with, 214; remainder removed from the East, 215

Cherokee Nation *vs.* State of Georgia, 210–11

Cheves, Langdon, exponent of broad constitutional construction, 159; President of United States Bank, 183

Chickasaw Indians, number, 203; location, 203; civilization, 203–204; removed, 214

Choctaw Indians, number, 203; location, 203; civilization, 203–204; removed, 214

Cincinnati greets Jackson, 115

Civil service, Adams and, 97–98; bibliography, 239; *see also* Spoils System

Claiborne, W. C. C., Governor-General and Intendant of Louisiana, 25

Clay, Henry, quoted, 43; and Jackson's Florida expedition, 62, 63; candidate for presi-

INDEX 243

Clay—*Continued*
dency (1824), 78, 82, 83, 84, 86, 87, 88; and Jackson, 80; "corrupt bargain," 89–92, 96; Secretary of State, 94, 97, 105; and nationalism, 100; loses hope of presidency, 109; Compromise Tariff, 179; and United States Bank, 189, 196; on veto power, 190; nominee of National Republican party (1832), 191, 225; on disposal of proceeds from public lands, 199; on removal of Indians, 215–16

Clayton, J. M., of Delaware, 148

Clinton, DeWitt, toasted at Tammany dinner, 64

Cochrane, Sir Alexander Inglis, Admiral, sends news of peace to Jackson, 46

Cocke, General John, 33, 34

Cohens *vs.* Virginia, 141

Columbia (S. C.), ordinance of nullification drawn up at, 170–71, 174

Columbian Observer of Philadelphia, 89, 90

Concord (N. H.), Jackson goes to, 219

Congress, question of Jackson's Florida expedition, 62–63; and Adams, 104–05; nationalistic laws, 138; Webster-Hayne debate, 145–57; Force Bill, 177, 179, 180; Verplanck Bill, 178; and United States Bank, 187, 189–91, 196; Senate censures Jackson, 196–98, 228; Senate ratifies Indian treaty, 206; creates Indian reservation, 209

Constitution, Adams for liberal construction, 99; amendment proposed, 105; questions in 1828, 143; Webster-Hayne debate, 145–57

Corn Tassel, Cherokee executed in Georgia, 212

Cotton, influence of price on sentiment of South Carolina, 159

Crawford, W. H., at Waxhaw settlement, 5; and Jackson, 62, 80; supported by Van Buren, 64; candidate for presidency, 76, 77, 81, 82, 83, 86; health fails, 83–84; supporters ally themselves to Jackson, 103

Creek Indians, and Tecumseh, 25; massacre at Fort Mims, 31, 32; outbreak in South, 32–36, 52, 54–55; treaty with, 37–38; number, 203; location, 203; civilization, 203; dispossessed, 205–07, 214; *see also* Creek War, Seminole War

Creek War, 32–38

Cumberland River, Jackson's army down the, 28

Dale, Sam, and Jackson, 174

Davie, W. R., Governor of North Carolina, 5

Democratic party, and United States Bank, 195; convention (1835), 225

Dickerson, Mahlon, of New Jersey, 148

Dickinson, Charles, killed in duel by Jackson, 21

Donelson, A. J., nephew and private secretary of Jackson, 114, 130

Donelson, Mrs. A. J., mistress of White House, 114, 221

Donelson, John, helps found Nashville, 12; Jackson marries daughter of, 15

Duane, W. J., Secretary of Treasury, 193–94

Earl, R. E. W., artist engaged in painting portraits of Jackson, 114

Eaton, J. H., and Jackson, 7–8, 52, 73, 116, 130; Secretary of War, 8, 117, 118, 208

Eaton, Mrs. J. H., 88, 132–34

Elections, Presidential, of 1824, 82–93, 95–96; manner of select-

INDEX

Elections—*Continued*
  ing President an issue of 1824, 84; "corrupt bargain," 89–92, 96; proposed amendment to Constitution providing direct, 105; campaign of 1828, 106–10; of 1832, 187, 191; of 1836, 226–27; of 1840, 232; of 1844, 233
England, frontiersman's attitude toward, 25; *see also* War of 1812
Everett, Edward, cited, 219

Finance, national debt paid, 199; Government funds in state banks, 199; independent treasury system, 199–200, 235; *see also* Bank, United States; Tariff
Florida and Jackson, 22, 27–28, 30–31, 39–40, 51–61; Southwest longs for conquest of, 26; encourages Indian uprising, 32; Spain and, 52, 53, 55–56, 61; controversy over Jackson's expedition, 61–64; United States treaty with Spain, 64
Foote, S. A., of Connecticut, 144
Force Bill, 177, 179; nullified by South Carolina convention, 180
Forsyth, John, of Georgia, 149
Fowltown, fight at, 54, 55
Franklin, "Western District" tries to set up State of, 12
Frelinghuysen, Theodore, of New Jersey, 148
Friends, Society of, protest removal of Indians, 216

Gaines, General E. P., 54, 55
Gallatin, Albert, Jackson makes acquaintance of, 17; describes Jackson, 18
Gazette, Nashville, 75
General Neville (river boat), Jackson travels down Ohio on, 101
Georgia, and state rights, 142; and tariff, 169; Indians of, 202, 203, 204, 205 *et seq.*; nullification, 213
Ghent, Treaty of, 43, 53, 137
Gibbs, General, 40
Girard Bank of Philadelphia, treasury receipts to be deposited in, 194
Globe, administration organ, 130, 230
Green, Duff, party manager for Jackson, 115; edits *United States Telegraph*, 118; in Kitchen Cabinet, 130
Grundy, Felix, of Tennessee, 74, 75, 149

Hall, D. A., Federal district judge in New Orleans, 47
Hamilton, J. A., 117, 118
Hamilton, James, Governor of South Carolina, 168, 170, 179
Harrisburg (Penn.), nominating convention at, 84
Harrison, W. H., Governor of Indiana, at Tippecanoe, 25; Jackson offers aid to, 26; resigns commission, 37; candidate for presidency, 226–27
Hartford Convention, 138
Harvard University confers degree on Jackson, 220
Havana, Jackson sends Spaniards to, 60
Hayne, R. Y., 110, 167; speech in Congress, 144–45; debate with Webster, 145–57; personal characteristics, 147; change in political ideas, 159, 163; and nullification, 162, 176; elected Governor of South Carolina, 172: biography, 239
Hermitage, The, Jackson's home, 19–20, 50, 55, 67, 68–72, 102–103, 218, 223, 231, 233, 234
Hill, Isaac, 111, 116, 221; Senate rejects nomination of, 129; in Kitchen Cabinet, 130; quoted, 164–65, 181

INDEX 245

Holmes, John, of Maine, 148
Horseshoe Bend, battle with Creeks at, 35
Houston, Sam, 35
Hunter's Hill, Jackson's plantation near Nashville, 15, 19
Huntsville (Ala.), Jackson brings forces together at, 33

Indian Queen Tavern (the Wigwam), 115, 120
Indian Territory created (1834), 214
Indians, 142; hostility near Nashville, 12; Creek War, 32–38; Seminole War, 54–58; removal of, 201–16, 236; *see also* names of tribes
Ingham, S. D., Secretary of Treasury, 117
Internal improvements, 138; Jackson on, 79; issue in 1824, 84; Adams and, 99, 100, 105; South opposes, 140; South Carolina and, 159; Maysville Road veto, 218

Jackson, Andrew, father of the President, 1–3
Jackson, Andrew, birth (1767), 3–4; birthplace, 4–5; early life, 5 *et seq.*; personal characteristics, 6, 7, 11, 15, 18, 19, 20–21, 213, 217, 234–35; education, 7, 10; in the Revolution, 8–9; attitude toward British, 9; business enterprises, 9–10, 19–20; in Charleston, 9–10; admitted to bar, 11; goes to Tennessee, 13–14; as "solicitor" in Nashville, 14–16; marriage, 15; represents Tennessee in Congress, 16–17; in Senate, 17–18, 69; as judge in Tennessee, 18–19; quarrels, 20–21; in War of 1812, 26 *et seq.*; nicknamed "Old Hickory," 30; in Creek War, 33–38; at

New Orleans, 40–43, 45–50; popularity, 45, 50, 63–64, 115, 210, 229–30; in Seminole War, and Florida expedition, 55–61; controversy about Florida expedition, 61–64; as Governor of Florida, 64–67; life at the Hermitage, 68–72, 102–03; candidate for presidency (1824), 73 *et seq.*, 95; and tariff, 79, 143, 162–63, 169, 235–36; and Adams, 80, 93–94, 108, 122, 220; and Crawford, 80; and Clay, 80; and Calhoun, 80, 134–35; candidate for presidency (1828), 100 *et seq.*; resigns from Senate, 102; as a politician, 107–08; election, 109–10; journey to Washington, 114–15; as President-elect, 115–19; Cabinet, 117–18, 129–30, 135–36, 193–194, 218; inauguration, 119–124; and Spoils System, 124–127, 236; and Congress, 128; Kitchen Cabinet, 130–31; Eaton controversy, 132–34; toast to the Union, 164–66; and nullification, 167, 173–77; candidate for reëlection (1832), 168, 218; proclamation to South Carolina (1832), 175–176; Force Bill, 177, 179, 180; and United States Bank, 182, 184 *et seq.*, 218; censured by Senate, 196–98, 228; and Indian policy, 208–09, 214–16; and Georgia, 213; journeys to New England, 219; Harvard confers degree on, 220; life at White House, 221–23; his finances, 223–24; political influence, 224–28; farewell address, 228–29; return to Nashville, 230; last years, 231–34; death (1845), 234; Webster's characterization of, 234–35; achievements, 235–36; bibliography, 237–38

INDEX

Jackson, Mrs. Andrew, mother of the President, 3-4, 5, 8-9

Jackson, Mrs. Andrew, wife of the President, 48-50, 65, 71, 122; quoted, 65-66, 68-69; death, 111-12

Jackson, Fort, 36; Treaty of, 54

Jamaica, British from, 40

Jefferson, Thomas, Jackson makes acquaintance of, 17; on Jackson, 18; candidate of the masses, 113; and State rights, 139, 141-42, 164

Jonesboro (Tenn.), Jackson's traveling party at, 13

Kemble, Fanny, and Jackson, 217

Kendall, Amos, 221; in Kitchen Cabinet, 130

Kentucky made a State (1791), 16

Key, F. S., at Jackson's inauguration, 121

King, W. R., of Alabama, 149

Kitchen Cabinet, 130-31

Knoxville (Tenn.), 25; convention at, 16

Kremer, George, and "corrupt bargain," 89-91

La Fayette, Marquis de, 219; and Jackson, 71-72

Lavasseur, secretary to La Fayette, 70

Lewis, Major W. B., 63, 125, 129, 134-35; campaign manager for Jackson, 74, 75, 85, 103, 111, 112, 163; accompanies Jackson to Washington, 114, 116, 221; in Kitchen Cabinet, 130

Livingston, Edward, 48; Jackson makes acquaintance of, 17; declines place in cabinet, 117; Secretary of State, 136; and proclamation to South Carolina, 175; and United States Bank, 188; minister to France, 193

Lodge, H. C., quoted, 146

Louisville greets Jackson, 115

Macay, Spruce, lawyer with whom Jackson studied, 10, 12

M'Culloch vs. Maryland (1819), 141, 183

MacDonald, William, *Jacksonian Democracy*, quoted, 152

McDuffie, George, 162, 189

McKemy family at whose home Jackson is said to have been born, 4

McLane, Louis, Secretary of Treasury, 136; and United States Bank, 188, 193

McLean, John, Postmaster-General, 118; candidate for presidency, 226

McNairy, John, 12-13, 14, 21

Mangum, W. P., of North Carolina, 227

Marshall, John, Chief-Justice, at Jackson's inauguration, 120, 121; and State rights, 138, 141; on Cherokee nation, 211; and Jackson, 213

Martinsville (N. C.), Jackson practices law at, 11

Mason, Jeremiah, branch bank president, 185

Maysville Road veto, 218

Mims, Fort (Ala.), massacre at, 31, 32, 36

Mississippi and Indians, 214

Mississippi Valley, British plan assault on, 38

Missouri Compromise, 159

Mobile, Jackson and, 29, 37, 39, 57; Congress authorizes taking of, 30

Monroe, Fortress, 173

Monroe, James, Secretary of War, 40; Jackson writes to, 43; and Jackson's Florida expedition, 56, 61, 62, 67; Jackson supports, 80; Adams confers with, 94; popular approval of, 95; and Indian question, 206

INDEX 247

Monticello, home of Jefferson, 18
Morganton (N. C.), 25; Jackson joins traveling party at, 13

Nashville (Tenn.), founded, 12; Jackson goes to, 13–14; in 1789, 14; Phillips reaches, 25; Jackson's army assembles at, 28; entertains Jackson, 37, 101; Jackson in, 51, 230
Natchez (Miss.), Jackson's troops in, 29, 30
National Intelligencer, 62, 89
National Republican party, 104, 108; defends United States Bank, 191, 195; joins Whigs, 225
Negro Fort, Nicholls's, 53, 54, 57
New England receives President Jackson, 219–20
New Orleans, news of War of 1812 reaches, 25; Jackson and, 28, 37, 39, 40–43, 45–50; gunboats sent from, 57
New Orleans Territory, Jackson denied governorship of, 20
New York (State) controls vice presidency, 75–76
New York City, fêtes Jackson, 63, 219; and nullification, 176
Nicholls, Colonel Edward, 32, 52–53
Nolte describes Jackson and his wife, 49–50
North Carolina, claims to be Jackson's birthplace, 4; and tariff, 169
Nullification, 161–80, 236; and Jefferson, 142; Georgia and, 142, 213; *South Carolina Exposition*, 142; Hayne on, 150; Webster on, 151, 152–53; Calhoun and, 161, 162, 164–165, 166, 167–68, 171, 172; Turnbull's *Crisis*, 161; Calhoun's *Exposition*, 161; Jackson and, 167, 173–77, 219; South Carolina's ordinance of, 170–171, 179–80; Force Bill, 177, 179, 180; Compromise Tariff, 178–79; bibliography, 239

Ohio on State rights, 141
O'Neil, "Peggy," *see* Eaton, Mrs. J. H.
O'Neil's Tavern, 87–88
Onis, Luis de, Spanish Minister, 61, 64
Oregon, Jackson desires extension in, 233
Osborn *vs.* United States Bank (1824), 183

Pakenham, General Sir Edward, 40, 42
Panama Congress (1826), 105
Parton, James, biographer of Jackson, 238; cited, 4, 18–19, 29, 72, 175
Peale, picture of Jackson by, 64
Pennsylvania, 193–94; grants Bank charter, 198
Pensacola, Jackson and, 29, 39, 40, 58; Nicholls at, 32; Spanish in, 52; toast to, 60
Philadelphia, national capital, 17; fêtes Jackson, 63, 219
Phillips, William, "Billy," courier, 23, 24–25, 26
Pickens, Andrew, at Waxhaw settlement, 5
Pittsburgh greets Jackson, 115
Poinsett, J. R., of South Carolina, 174
Political parties, no party lines in 1822, 76; *see also* Democratic, National Republican, Republican, Whig
Polk, J. K., 230, 233
Public lands, Adams and, 99; Foote's resolution (1829), 144–145, 155; sale of, 169, 199

Randolph, John, 17, 93, 96
"Red Sticks," name for Creek braves, 36, 54

INDEX

Reid, John, biographer of Jackson, 7
Republican party, and Constitution, 99; supports Jackson, 103
Rhea, John, 56, 74
"Rhea letter," 56
Richmond Enquirer, 141
Roane, Judge, of Virginia, 141
Robertson, James, helps found Nashville, 12
Rush, Richard, cited, 61

St. Augustine, Jackson and, 29; Spaniards in, 52
St. Marks, Spaniards in, 52; Jackson and, 57, 58
Salisbury (N. C.), 25; Jackson studies law at, 10–11
Scott, General Winfield, 173, 215
Scott, Fort, 55, 57
Seminole Indians, 52
Seminole War, 54–58
Sevier, John, Governor of Tennessee, 20
Seymour, Horatio, of Vermont, 148
Slavery, South resists federal legislation on, 140
South, The, on State rights, 139–140, 143; and United States Bank, 140; and tariff, 160–61; *see also* names of States
South Carolina, claims to be birthplace of Jackson, 4; and tariff, 142, 145, 159, 166; *see also* Nullification
South Carolina Exposition, 142
"Southwest Territory," 16
Spain, and Florida, 52, 53, 55–56; treaty with, 64; *see also* Florida
Spoils System, Jackson and, 124–27, 236
State rights, 139–40; Hayne on, 150, 154; Webster on, 152; *see also* Nullification
Story, Judge Joseph, quoted, 123
Strother, Fort, 34, 35

Supreme Court, on State rights, 138–39; on United States Bank, 133; on Indian rights, 210–12; Georgia defies, 212–213
Suwanee (Fla.), Jackson at, 58
Swann, Thomas, Jackson and, 21

Tammany entertains Jackson, 63
Taney, R. B., Attorney-General, 136; writes for Jackson, 190, 228; Secretary of Treasury, 194, 196
Tariff, 84, 158 *et seq*.; Jackson and, 79, 143, 162–63, 169, 235–36; Adams and, 99; Calhoun votes for protection, 139; South opposes protective, 140, 142, 143, 159–60; woolens bill (1827), 160; Act of 1824, 160, 161; Act of 1828, 160, 169, 170; Act of 1832, 169, 170; Force Bill, 177, 179, 180; Verplanck Bill, 178; Compromise Tariff, 179; bibliography, 239; *see also* Nullification
Tecumseh works among Southern Indians, 25–26
Tennessee, admitted as State (1796), 16; meaning of name, 16; Legislature favors Jackson's nomination, 102; Indians, 202
Texas, Jackson favors annexation, 235
Tippecanoe, Battle of, 25
Tohopeka, battle at, 35
Troup, G. M., Governor of Georgia, 206
Turnbull, R. J., *The Crisis*, 161
Turner, F. J., *The Rise of the New West*, quoted, 159–60
Twelve-mile Creek, Jackson's father settles on, 2
Tyler, John, President, 148; Bank vetoes, 200

Union County (N. C.), Jackson's father settles in, 3

ID# INDEX

United States Telegraph, of Washington, Jackson organ, 102, 118, 130

Van Buren, Martin, 63, 115, 219, 221, 232, 233; supports Jackson, 103–04; Governor of New York, 116–17; Secretary of State, 117, 118; in Kitchen Cabinet, 130; aims at presidency, 132–34, 135; in Eaton controversy, 133–34; appointment as minister to Great Britain not ratified, 136; advises Jackson, 166; candidate for vice presidency, 168, 224; sets up independent treasury system, 200; candidate for presidency, 224–25; election, 226–27; inauguration, 230; biography, 238
Verplanck, J. C., of New York, tariff bill, 178
Virginia, controls presidency, 75–76; and State rights, 141–142; and tariff, 169

War of 1812, 24 *et seq.*, 52, 99, 137–38
Washington, George, 14, 219
Washington, captured, 38; Jackson journeys to, 50–51, 85, 114–15
Waxhaw settlement, Jackson family at, 2; notable people from, 5; in the Revolution, 8
Weathersford, Creek half-breed, 36
Webster, Daniel, 18, 93, 189, 196; quoted, 115–16, 127; constitutional debate (1830), 145–57; life and characteristics, 147–148; Jackson's estimate of, 225–26; on Jackson, 234–35; bibliography, 238
Webster, Ezekiel, 113
West, The, and War of 1812, 25; and Indian policy, 201 *et seq.*
"Western District" tries to set up State, 12
Whig party, 225; tries to resurrect United States Bank, 200
White, H. L., of Tennessee, 116, 149; candidate for presidency, 224, 226, 227
Wilkinson, General James, 29, 31, 37
Wirt, William, 210
Woodbury, Levi, Secretary of Navy, 136, 148, 219
Worcester *vs.* State of Georgia, 211–12

AN OUTLINE OF THE PLAN OF
THE CHRONICLES OF AMERICA

The fifty titles of the Series fall into eight topical sequences or groups, each with a dominant theme of its own—

I. *The Morning of America*
TIME: 1492-1763

THE theme of the first sequence is the struggle of nations for the possession of the New World. The mariners of four European kingdoms—Spain, Portugal, France, and England—are intent upon the discovery of a new route to Asia. They come upon the American continent which blocks the way. Spain plants colonies in the south, lured by gold. France, in pursuit of the fur trade, plants colonies in the north. Englishmen, in search of homes and of a wider freedom, occupy the Atlantic seaboard. These Englishmen come in time to need the land into which the French have penetrated by way of the St. Lawrence and the Great Lakes, and a mighty struggle between the two nations takes place in the wilderness, ending in the expulsion of the French. This sequence comprises ten volumes:

1. THE RED MAN'S CONTINENT, *by Ellsworth Huntington*
2. THE SPANISH CONQUERORS, *by Irving Berdine Richman*
3. ELIZABETHAN SEA-DOGS, *by William Wood*
4. CRUSADERS OF NEW FRANCE, *by William Bennett Munro*
5. PIONEERS OF THE OLD SOUTH, *by Mary Johnston*
6. THE FATHERS OF NEW ENGLAND, *by Charles M. Andrews*
7. DUTCH AND ENGLISH ON THE HUDSON, *by Maud Wilder Goodwin*
8. THE QUAKER COLONIES, *by Sydney G. Fisher*
9. COLONIAL FOLKWAYS, *by Charles M. Andrews*
10. THE CONQUEST OF NEW FRANCE, *by George M. Wrong*

II. The Winning of Independence
TIME: 1763-1815

The French peril has passed, and the great territory between the Alleghanies and the Mississippi is now open to the Englishmen on the seaboard, with no enemy to contest their right of way except the Indian. But the question arises whether these Englishmen in the New World shall submit to political dictation from the King and Parliament of England. To decide this question the War of the Revolution is fought; the Union is born: and the second war with England follows. Seven volumes:

11. THE EVE OF THE REVOLUTION, *by Carl Becker*
12. WASHINGTON AND HIS COMRADES IN ARMS, *by George M. Wrong*
13. THE FATHERS OF THE CONSTITUTION, *by Max Farrand*
14. WASHINGTON AND HIS COLLEAGUES, *by Henry Jones Ford*
15. JEFFERSON AND HIS COLLEAGUES, *by Allen Johnson*
16. JOHN MARSHALL AND THE CONSTITUTION, *by Edward S. Corwin*
17. THE FIGHT FOR A FREE SEA, *by Ralph D. Paine*

III. The Vision of the West
TIME: 1750-1890

The theme of the third sequence is the American frontier—the conquest of the continent from the Alleghanies to the Pacific Ocean. The story covers nearly a century and a half, from the first crossing of the Alleghanies by the backwoodsmen of Pennsylvania, Virginia, and the Carolinas (about 1750) to the heyday of the cowboy on the Great Plains in the latter part of the nineteenth century. This is the marvelous tale of the greatest migrations in history, told in nine volumes as follows:

18. PIONEERS OF THE OLD SOUTHWEST, *by Constance Lindsay Skinner*
19. THE OLD NORTHWEST, *by Frederic Austin Ogg*
20. THE REIGN OF ANDREW JACKSON, *by Frederic Austin Ogg*
21. THE PATHS OF INLAND COMMERCE, *by Archer B. Hulbert*
22. ADVENTURERS OF OREGON, by *Constance Lindsay Skinner*
23. THE SPANISH BORDERLANDS, *by Herbert E. Bolton*
24. TEXAS AND THE MEXICAN WAR, *by Nathaniel W. Stephenson*
25. THE FORTY-NINERS, *by Stewart Edward White*
26. THE PASSING OF THE FRONTIER, *by Emerson Hough*

IV. *The Storm of Secession*
TIME: 1830-1876

The curtain rises on the gathering storm of secession. The theme of the fourth sequence is the preservation of the Union, which carries with it the extermination of slavery. Six volumes as follows:

27. THE COTTON KINGDOM, *by William E. Dodd*
28. THE ANTI-SLAVERY CRUSADE, *by Jesse Macy*
29. ABRAHAM LINCOLN AND THE UNION, *by Nathaniel W. Stephenson*
30. THE DAY OF THE CONFEDERACY, *by Nathaniel W. Stephenson*
31. CAPTAINS OF THE CIVIL WAR, *by William Wood*
32. THE SEQUEL OF APPOMATTOX, *by Walter Lynwood Fleming*

V. *The Intellectual Life*

Two volumes follow on the higher national life, telling of the nation's great teachers and interpreters:

33. THE AMERICAN SPIRIT IN EDUCATION, *by Edwin E. Slosson*
34. THE AMERICAN SPIRIT IN LITERATURE, *by Bliss Perry*

VI. *The Epic of Commerce and Industry*

The sixth sequence is devoted to the romance of industry and business, and the dominant theme is the transformation caused by the inflow of immigrants and the development and utilization of mechanics on a great scale. The long age of muscular power has passed, and the era of mechanical power has brought with it a new kind of civilization. Eight volumes:

35. OUR FOREIGNERS, *by Samuel P. Orth*
36. THE OLD MERCHANT MARINE, *by Ralph D. Paine*
37. THE AGE OF INVENTION, *by Holland Thompson*
38. THE RAILROAD BUILDERS, *by John Moody*
39. THE AGE OF BIG BUSINESS, *by Burton J. Hendrick*
40. THE ARMIES OF LABOR, *by Samuel P. Orth*
41. THE MASTERS OF CAPITAL, *by John Moody*
42. THE NEW SOUTH, *by Holland Thompson*

VII. *The Era of World Power*

The seventh sequence carries on the story of government and diplomacy and political expansion from the Reconstruction (1876) to the present day, in six volumes:

43. THE BOSS AND THE MACHINE, *by Samuel P. Orth*
44. THE CLEVELAND ERA, *by Henry Jones Ford*
45. THE AGRARIAN CRUSADE, *by Solon J. Buck*
46. THE PATH OF EMPIRE, *by Carl Russell Fish*
47. THEODORE ROOSEVELT AND HIS TIMES, *by Harold Howland*
48. WOODROW WILSON AND THE WORLD WAR, *by Charles Seymour*

VIII. *Our Neighbors*

Now to round out the story of the continent, the Hispanic peoples on the south and the Canadians on the north are taken up where they were dropped further back in the Series, and these peoples are followed down to the present day:

49. THE CANADIAN DOMINION, *by Oscar D. Skelton*
50. THE HISPANIC NATIONS OF THE NEW WORLD, *by William R. Shepherd*

The Chronicles of America is thus a great synthesis, giving a new projection and a new interpretation of American History. These narratives are works of real scholarship, for every one is written after an exhaustive examination of the sources. Many of them contain new facts; some of them —such as those by Howland, Seymour, and Hough—are founded on intimate personal knowledge. But the originality of the Series lies, not chiefly in new facts, but rather in new ideas and new combinations of old facts.

The General Editor of the Series is Dr. Allen Johnson, Chairman of the Department of History of Yale University, and the entire work has been planned, prepared, and published under the control of the Council's Committee on Publications of Yale University.

Ross & Perry, Inc.
Publishers
216 G Street, N.E.
Washington, D.C. 20002
Telephone: (202) 675-8300
Facsimile: (202) 675-8400

www.ingramcontent.com/pod-product-compliance
Lightning Source LLC
Chambersburg PA
CBHW030239170426
43202CB00007B/59